RELIGIOUS LIFE
AT THE CROSSROADS

RELIGIOUS LIFE
AT THE CROSSROADS

edited by
David A. Fleming, S.M.

PAULIST PRESS
New York/Mahwah

248,27
F

Acknowledgments

The Publisher gratefully acknowledges the permission by *Review for Religious* for the use of "Trends in Religious Life Today" by John M. Lozano, C.M.F. (Vol. 42, July/August 1983, pp. 481–505), and by the Conference of Major Superiors of Men (CMSM) for the following articles:

"Hope-Filled Deeds and Critical Thought" (CMSM Presentation to Third Inter-American Conference of Religious, Montreal, 1977)

"The Role of U.S. Religious in Human Promotion" by Barbara Kraemer, O.S.F.; Phil Land, S.J.; Joan Puls, O.S.F. (1980)

"Pilgrims and Prophets" (CMSM Presentation to Fourth Inter-American Conference of Religious, Santiago, 1980)

"In Solidarity and Service" (CMSM Task Force on Clericalism, 1983)

"The Church in the United States as Prophet" by John A. Grindel, C.M. (1983)

"Our Search for God" (Boston Annual Assembly, 1983)

"Religious Leadership in a Time of Cultural Change" by Thomas E. Clarke, S.J. (1984)

"Afterword" by Ron Carignan, O.M.I. (1984)

Library of Congress
Catalog Card Number: 85-60288

ISBN: 0-8091-2709-1

Published by Paulist P
997 Macarthur Boulev
Mahwah, N.J. 07430

Printed and bound in
United States of America

Distributed by...

MARIANIST COMMUNICATION CENTER
1223 MARYHURST DRIVE
ST. LOUIS, MISSOURI 63122-7229
PHONE (314) 965-5634

CONTENTS

INTRODUCTION

David A. Fleming, S.M.

The past decade has witnessed a considerable evolution in the understanding and experience of life in Roman Catholic canonical religious communities throughout the world. This evolution has been quite evident in the United States.

During these years, the Conference of Major Superiors of Men has understood its role as one of stimulating reflection and assisting major superiors of religious communities to provide leadership at a critical moment in the history of their Institutes. Throughout this period, the CMSM has worked closely at these tasks with the Leadership Conference of Women Religious of the United States and the National Conference of Catholic Bishops.

The present volume is a collection of landmark essays and addresses which touch on themes that have characterized the work of the Conference during the past ten years. With one exception, all the essays, addresses, and articles in this book were solicited by the CMSM as a part of its ongoing ministry to major superiors.

Nevertheless, this book cannot in any way be considered a statement of official positions by the Conference. Some of the items included here fall into the category of provocative stimulus. Others were much appreciated reflections of speakers at National Assemblies. Others attempt to summarize a general state of mind or position congenial to the majority of members of the Conference. The papers published in the name of the Conference for the Inter-American meetings of 1977 and 1980 are those which were prepared with the greatest amount of consultation of the membership.

This volume has been prepared by the members of the Religious Life and Ministry Committee (Martin J. Kirk, C.M.F., Chairperson; Wilfrid Dewan, C.S.P.; David A. Fleming, S.M.; Cornelius Hubbuch, C.F.X.; Lawrence Madden, S.J.). We hope that it will be of interest not only to men religious in the United States, but, more broadly, to those interested in the renewal of religious life everywhere.

1

THE PAST AS PROLOGUE

John W. Padberg, S.J.

The Annual Assembly of the Conference of Major Superiors of Men in San Francisco in August 1976 was a significant meeting, enunciating key themes which were to exert a long-term influence on the work of the Conference.

Father Padberg's presentation on the history of religious life in the United States and its implications for today was particularly provocative. Over the years, this paper has continued to serve as a guideline to the members of the Conference in their efforts at self-understanding and renewal.

Father Padberg is a specialist in Church history and is the President of Weston School of Theology, Cambridge, Massachusetts.

I. INTRODUCTION

I would like to start by stating quite simply what I hope to accomplish here. I mean to explore the particular or special mission of religious orders and congregations in the United States over the last two centuries. Since this reflection has been requested by the Conference of Major Superiors of Men, I shall devote myself especially to male orders, although women's are at least equally important to the historian.

Why this topic? First, as a contribution to the understanding of our "heritage"; second, as a prologue to future reflection on our "vision"; third, because I like to tell some good stories; lastly, because as an historian I would like to offer these reflections as a context for the reflections, deliberations and decisions of major religious superiors. George Santayana's remark that he who does not live the past is fated to repeat it has in itself been repeated often enough to become achingly familiar. But that does not diminish the truth of the saying, and while there are many things from the past that would indeed bear repeating, there are others which we might at least try our best to avoid.

While my subject is the special mission of religious orders and congregations in the United States over the last two centuries, space does not permit me to deal here and now with their internal spiritual life, nor their internal community life. I am going to approach that subject with a particular organizing idea about our work over the last two centuries. That organizing idea came out of my research into and reflections upon this present subject and it can be stated quite directly. It is the following: religious congregations in the United States over the last two centuries had the particular characteristics of breaking ground and innovating in response to particular or new or special needs of the Church, that then, when those responses were most successful, they institutionalized the responses. They were able to be thus innovative, to provide a hospitable climate for new and familiar ideas and actions in the apostolate, for the entrepreneur and the maverick, because they had the old familiar structures of support in a rigid community life. Often, however, it was precisely that community life which later pushed them into over-institutionalizing the new ventures. I know that this is a very broad statement, and as Samuel Johnson once said, "I have here risen to the grandeur of generalizations." I shall, however, later try to get to the quirky qualifications, the unexpected possibilities and the vivid surprises that would qualify such a general treatment in itself.

In fact I shall use and try to combine two words which are currently sacrosanct vocables, one in the American and the other in the religious context. Those two words which thus describe the particular characteristic of religious orders are that they had a *frontier charism*. To that I would add a third word, not in such good repute today, and that is the word *institutionalized*. They institutionalized the results of that charism.

It is obviously impossible to do a full chronological treatment of the history of religious orders as I more than once in college or university courses attempted to do a history of Western civilization from Adam to Truman and from the womb to the tomb. This will not be a treatment from the Desert to the Golden Gate Bridge. Rather, I shall try to take several model examples and put them within a chronological framework. Those models, first of all, will come from the very remote past. Secondly, the models will contain a series of vignettes from the United States' religious history. They will combine past and present facts as a prologue to your own future decisions and actions.

Before I get to the question of this background, let me say a word more about what I mean by a frontier charism. As a diocesan structure ideally works in a set place and within established patterns, for the good of the community of the Church, so, it seems to me, a religious order structure ideally is working in no one particular set place and is working within new patterns which have been discovered or invented.

Because of this mobility and diversity, both geographical and psychological, the religious order has to have a community structure and an operative myth strong enough to support its members and to bring them to undertake what are, at times, very difficult things in the fulfillment of their apostolate. What this translates into in the course of the orders and congregations in American Church history we shall see somewhat later.

II. BACKGROUND

I said I would not go back to Adam. I shall, however, now go back at least to a few illustrative examples from pre-American Church history. After that I shall try to go forward to the late eighteenth and the early nineteenth centuries when religious first came to America in significant numbers.

Each of these examples illustrates a new response to a particular need, and I shall attempt to put each of them in the form of a question and an answer, followed by a brief comment on evolving characteristics.

The first new or special need to which the first coherently organized body of religious responded was quite simply: How, as a passionately convinced believer, does one come to terms with a Church increasingly inserted into the contemporary world of the fourth century, a Church which was getting comfortably institutionalized in that world after Constantine had made all of us ragtag early-Christian-rabble finally and fully legitimate? The answer to that came in the example of the radical renunciation of the world undertaken by the Desert Fathers. It was done, as any such action is done, in a particular context and in a particular place. The place was the desert of Egypt and the context was that of a world-renouncing neo-Platonic philosophy. I suppose some of us through many years have been mildly amused or sometimes irritated by the chapters in Rodriguez' *Practice of Perfection and Christian Virtue* in which "the previous teaching is confirmed by examples." But perhaps we should, with an historian's eye, take those examples more seriously than we have. In any case the first manifestation of religious life in the Church involved a public commitment on the part of individuals, to the exigencies, the demands, of the Gospel. It was a commitment on the part of individuals, sometimes very cantankerous individuals, who originally had very little idea of forming a community but who were rather interested in gathering as individuals around a teacher on the way of perfection.

The second question was: How would Christians respond at the time of the barbarian invasions to the breakdown of the fabric of a civilization into which the Church had progressively been building itself and of which it was becoming part and parcel? The answer was monasticism, and especially Benedictine monasticism which brought to at least a fragment of the Church and to a fragment of the society in which it existed order and stability. However often some of the abbeys and monasteries through the many centuries needed reform and however lurid some of the stories of the monasteries of the time were, the Church at that time often needed reform even more. The Benedictine monasteries and abbeys from the fifth to the twelfth centuries were oases of piety, order, stability and devotion in a world which seemed increasingly impious, disordered, unstable and practically, if not ideologically, irreligious. As the great monastic historian Leclerc said in entitling one of his books, these places were the locale of "the love of learning and the desire for God."

Monasticism advanced one great step on the characteristic I had mentioned at the end of the first vignette. Here we had not only the public commitment to the Gospel exigencies on the part of individuals but on the part of whole communities with the recognition by the Church as such. The most conspicuous examples of this, of course, would be Cluniac Benedictinism and the Cistercian foundations.

The Church next had to ask itself how it would respond to an urban, mercantile, mobile, newly rich civilization of the late Middle Ages, the thirteenth century, for example, a civilization to the worldliness of which many churchmen often succumbed. The answer was the mendicant orders, most obviously the Dominican and the Franciscan, and, somewhat earlier as a bridge, the Canons Regular, the most prominent of whom were the Norbertines or Praemonstratensians. Here religious orders did two absolutely important things. First, they appropriated the new (and supposedly subversive) learning of Aristotle to the service of the Gospel. (We do not realize how Aristotle was the Darwin, Marx, and Freud of his day, all wrapped in one.) Second, they recalled to Christians the basic virtues of simplicity, renunciation, and piety. Here again there was a love of learning and the desire for God. It was again expressed by people gathered in communities and as community ventures, but now in such groups which were increasingly mobile and directly apostolic.

How did the Church respond several centuries later to the anthropocentric humanism of the Renaissance and to the sometimes legitimate, sometimes illegitimate clamor for reform that led to the breaking of Church unity in the Reformation? How respond also to the increasing individualism emphasized by both movements? The answer was in the Clerics Regular and the directly apostolic orders, among them, for example, the Jesuits and the Theatines. Here there was a frank acceptance of the secular learning of the time, the establishment of religious communities which in their militancy and vigor equaled the vigor of the Protestant reformers. There was the cultivation of individual piety and devotions for the highly individualistic men of the times. More importantly, these communities not only were mobile and directly apostolic, but they made a public commitment to apostolates in the institutionalized secular realm, for example in schools, educational institutions set up apart from their own communities. The seeds of "separate incorporation" were already sown in the sixteenth and seventeenth centuries.

To move out of a European context, how did particular groups in the Church respond to the new worlds opened up to the Gospel by the great age of exploration? In some ways the finding in the old world of Asia and the new world of America of non-Christian millions, to whom the preaching of the Gospel had been an impossibility, raised questions as profound for the Church as the finding of human beings on the moon would have raised in our own day in the first space landings there. The answer again was in the religious orders and the missionary endeavors. It may come as a surprise to us, but the first large-scale organized missionary enterprise in the history of the Church took place as recently as the beginning of the sixteenth century. Those endeavors were organized by the religious orders themselves long before they were organized by the universal Church acting through the Roman curia and the papacy. For the first time the apostolates of religious orders were organized on a large scale for non-Christians.

Lastly, how did particular groups in the Church respond to the recognition of the need for increasingly specialized apostolates in a world growing increasingly specialized? An example: the need of education for women and for the poor. The answer: such special character schools as those originally founded by the Ursulines or by the Christian Brothers and for which apostolate they were explicitly set up. Of course, the women with original institutional ideas were often forced by men back into pre-conceived models, as with Angela Merici or Mary Ward or Jane de Chantal. Those stories need telling and re-telling, of how good and holy men were often simply blind to the visions seen by extraordinary women religious.

Each of these needs was a particular and special need at a particular time and in special circumstances in the Church. Each elicited a particular response. All of them, however, responded at the same time to some universal regularly recurrent needs for any group which would coherently organize itself in the service of the Church. Those constant needs were: first, a commitment to the exigencies of the Gospel, a commitment to a response which was not only individual but communitarian, a public acceptance by the Church, and increasingly the awareness of the help which this community brought not only to its own members but to the wider community of the Church in and through specific apostolates. Almost always these were responses to very large needs.

In some cases, however, there were even very particular needs to which the foundation of religious orders responded. For example, there was an order in France in the late Middle Ages which had as its apostolate the building or rebuilding of bridges—and I mean literal, not figurative, bridges. It is the acknowledged ancestor of the department of national highways in France.

So much for our background. I must admit the speed with which we have covered these vignettes is something like traveling in a 747 six thousand feet above the ground at about five hundred miles per hour across the United States. The impression can be rather blurred.

Let us then turn to the United States as the religious orders came here. Briefly, I think that many of the general characteristics of historical development of orders were present here, too.

III. RELIGIOUS ORDERS IN THE UNITED STATES

When I first began to do research to prepare the material for this presentation, it quickly became obvious that the subject was not one of such burning interest that a lot of people felt compelled to write on it. In the last ten years, at least according to the Guide to Catholic

Periodical Literature, there has been on the subject only one article, and that one, in *The Jurist,* had the title "The Bishops versus the Religious Orders: The Suppressed Decrees of the Third Plenary Council of Baltimore." There is a fruitful field for doctoral dissertations on the part of any young aspiring historians.

To what new needs did the religious orders in the United States respond? At the beginning they were the same ones as in the old world of the sixteenth and seventeenth centuries. There was the generalized missionary endeavor of seeking out new worlds for the Gospel, and this was true of people as diverse as Andrew White when he came in 1634 on the Ark and Dove to Maryland as it was of Kino in Arizona in the seventeenth century. It was true of Serra in California and Jogues in New York. It was true of Hennepin in Minnesota and Rale in Maine, all members of religious orders. In each case this first or initial seeking of new worlds to be converted to the Gospel, new people to be brought to the knowledge of our Lord, was initiated by members of religious orders, not by members of the structured diocesan clergy who as yet had no structure in this country.

In the eighteenth century, in the southwest, Spanish-speaking priests out of Mexico institutionalized that drive for conversion through the glorious missions such as we see still strung out like a rosary through California. In the midwest, through the Ohio and Mississippi valleys, it was most often the French religious clergy out of Quebec.

Very often this response came on the part of individual members of those orders. They were entrepreneurs, heroes, or operators, depending upon your point of view and upon what they did. But besides being individuals, they were sustained internally and externally by their orders—internally by the personal sense of belonging to a group which supported them and externally by the institutional structures of the order upon which ultimately they could rely.

In that same eighteenth century, before the American Revolution, with so few Catholics in what was to become the United States— only thirty thousand of them—and with so much anti-Catholic bigotry, it was difficult enough just to hold the Church together. That was done most often by a few members of the clergy in Philadelphia or in Pennsylvania and in Maryland.

It is hard for us to recognize how very small the Church was at the beginning of our existence as a nation. In 1776 out of about three million people in the thirteen original colonies, there were only about thirty thousand Catholics, one percent of the population. Roughly one hundred years later, in 1870, there were four and a half million Catholics out of thirty-three million people, more than thirteen and a half percent. In the first hundred years of our history, while the United States population as a whole increased elevenfold, the Catholic population on the other hand multiplied itself one hundred and fifty times.

The anti-Catholic bigotry of the eighteenth century is also hard for us to recall. The "whore of Babylon" and the "harlot of Rome" were common enough compliments for the Church. A slide presentation of the vicious cartoons regularly published in the nineteenth century would be surprising to most of us.

If we look back at the Church in the United States when it was established juridically with the appointment and consecration of Bishop John Carroll, it had a few priests and some Catholics, and an immense amount of misunderstanding; but its biggest problem, its most striking liability, was that there were literally no ecclesiastical institutions other than a few scattered parishes. The first great contribution of the religious congregations to the history of Catholicism in the United States in the last two hundred years has been the building up of an infra-structure of institutions. Other than the dioceses and parishes themselves, every other institution by which the Church has been propagated in the United States was originally the work of religious congregations.

In education the primary schools, parochial and private, are the totally unique accomplishment, the incredible achievement of the religious orders of women, beginning with Elizabeth Seton and going on to the dozens of other foundresses. In secondary education the high schools were founded by members of religious congregations—for example, the Christian Brothers or the Society of Mary or the Xaverian Brothers. Higher education got off the ground at the instigation of the religious orders, in largest number most notably the women's religious orders, and, among the men, such groups as the Jesuits and the Congregation of the Holy Cross. Primary and secondary education, higher education, orphanages, hospitals, retreat houses, centers of spirituality, spiritual and apostolic movements such as the Sodality or the Apostleship of Prayer were all religious order foundations. Most of the

Catholic publications in the United States, other than diocesan newspapers, were also founded by religious, and examples come easily to mind, such as *Sign* of the Passionists, *Ave Maria* of the Congregation of the Holy Cross, *America* of the Society of Jesus, and *The Catholic World* of the Paulists. All of these became over two centuries part of the infra-structure of institutions.

Let me give from the eighteenth, nineteenth and twentieth centuries a few vignettes of the establishment of these institutionalized means for the promotion of the faith.

From the eighteenth century, the first of them I would talk about is the educational structure. Already in 1786 there were plans for a school for young men. In 1789 Georgetown received its foundation charter from the Congress of the United States. Its first personnel were members of the diocesan clergy in Maryland, former members of the Society of Jesus which by then had been suppressed for some sixteen years. In July 1791, the first permanent educational foundation in the United States by a religious order was established when four Sulpicians and five students came to found St. Mary's Seminary in Baltimore. In that same year Georgetown started its first classes with exactly one student. One year later the school, obviously responding to a need, had sixty-six students. That clergy had recognized a fact and responded to a need of the Catholic population. By 1795 Carroll's small band of priests in the United States was supplemented by the arrival of the Augustinians in Philadelphia where they took up parish work.

Moving then to the early nineteenth century, a second vignette would simply be the frontier interest exhibited by the early religious orders. Already in 1805 the Dominicans had established St. Rose Priory in Springfield, Kentucky, and Kentucky was way out on the western frontier in the terms of those days. In 1812 the diocesan priest, Nerinckx, had established what came to be the Sisters of Loretto in Kentucky, and the Sulpician priest, David, in the same year helped to establish the Sisters of Charity of Nazareth, again in Kentucky. By the 1820's the beginnings of missionary work among the Indians of the west took place. One example of that would be the arrival in 1823 at Florissant near St. Louis of a small group of Jesuits who had come from Belgium. The Maryland Jesuits were too poor to support them, and after floating down the Ohio and walking up the banks of the Mississippi, they arrived to start their work among the Indian tribes of the west, and one order after another entered into that apostolate.

A third, and even more important, vignette from the middle and later nineteenth century deals with the Church's response to immigration. The trickles of immigrants in the late eighteenth and early nineteenth centuries turned into a stream in the 1840's and 1850's and reached flood proportions in the later nineteenth century. The first and older immigration had been Irish and German. While this continued, the new immigration came from Eastern and Southern Europe among the Italians, the Polish, and the Slovaks, to name just a few groups. In 1900 there were twelve million Catholics in the United States, triple that of thirty years before.

Central to maintaining the faith of the millions of immigrants flocking in upon the Church was the foundation of parishes in which they could at one and the same time find familiar supports of the faith and be introduced to its life and practice in the new American environment. There plainly and simply were not enough members of the diocesan clergy to take care of such parishes. As for the ethnic clergy who might have come from the same traditional background as the immigrants, nowhere did they exist in any appreciable numbers in the dioceses of the United States. At this point the religious orders played a most important role in the foundation and maintenance of such immigrant parishes. To take the example of Chicago alone, as Andrew Greeley has recently pointed out, the Redemptorists and the Benedictines were highly instrumental in the foundation of German parishes, the Benedictines in the foundation of Bohemian and Czech parishes, the Congregation of the Holy Cross in Polish parishes, the Franciscans and the Scalabrini Fathers in Italian parishes, the Jesuits in what for a time was the largest parish in North America, Holy Family Parish, for Irish immigrants. All of this was an institutional response to a new need—the preservation of the faith among an immigrant group. It was a need which could not have been met without an institutionalization of insight. Most often this was the insight of certain individual members of these orders. They sometimes had a lonely road on which to begin to march, but however successful they were in founding a parish, they would never have been able to carry on its multifarious activities without the support of the order or congregation to which they belonged. There is a striking example, of course, of an order which itself as a new American foundation sought to institutionalize the insights gained from the particular American experience. They were and are the Paulists, and Isaac Hecker, their founder, could never have succeeded so brilliantly were it not for the support of the men who joined him as they formed that community.

A fourth vignette from the late nineteenth and early twentieth centuries: As one wave of immigration succeeded the other, the earlier immigrants began to have the opportunity for something simply beyond mere survival. Diocesan structure answered the need with parishes. The need for education was met by the religious orders of women with the parochial schools. As I said earlier, all the educational endeavors of the Church in the United States through the nineteenth century, with few exceptions, were the work of religious orders. The need was quite evident. It was the necessity for the insertion of Catholic talent into the mainstream of American life. Often enough the response originally began as an entrepreneurial venture of certain individuals, both men and women. More than one Catholic school in the United States, primary, secondary or collegiate, was founded by an individual who received the spiritual resource of an explicit task or mission to found a school and no material resources whatever other than perhaps train fare to the school's city.

Indeed as recently as fifty years ago at least one important professional school of a major Catholic university in the United States was founded with the injunction of the rector of the university to a particular priest to go ahead and start the school, with two small rooms in one of the oldest buildings of the university and with fifty cents to buy stationery until the print shop could make up a letterhead. As for entrepreneurs, at least one province of the Society of Jesus in the United States got started when a Jesuit missionary in another area, with what might be excess of initiative, simply took off from that area which he regarded as somewhat stagnant and headed for fields which, as he wrote to the astonished superior of the mother province in Europe upon which the mission depended, were more "ripe for the harvest."

That educational endeavor started with colleges which in some instances quickly became universities. Originally there were few or no separate high schools because that entity as a particular stage in the American educational process had not yet entered the scene, but when high schools did become a common feature in America, the religious orders—for example, the Marianists, the Viatorians, and others who had not in previous years been engaged in a directly educational apostolate—took them on.

The fifth and last vignette deals with the middle and more recent twentieth century where increasingly education, in the sense of the encouragement of higher research and social concerns, entered upon the American scene. As research grew in the educational enterprise in the United States in the 1930's and 1940's and especially after the Second World War, there was almost no institutional involvement by the Church in the United States in research upon its own opportunities and problems. What little there was in most instances was done in the area of theological scholarship by people most often in the theological seminaries run by the religious orders. Even religious orders have until very recently done little research into themselves. CARA is an all too recent and very needed arrival on the scene. It is instructive to note, too, that it was only in the 1940's that the incredibly large, rich and well-organized American Church even began regularly to support even a single journal of theological scholarship, *Theological Studies*. As for social concern, here too the pattern was of individual entrepreneurs beginning to work in such things as labor schools or in sensitive areas of labor relations, often with little or no institutional commitment on the part of any of the organized entities in the Church. Some there was from particular religious orders and a little there was in conjunction with the colleges or universities run by such orders.

So much for vignettes. They were all stories of accomplishments. As Andrew Greeley has said, "The pre-1960 Church died of its own accomplishments." We ought also to talk a bit about some of the failures, the missed opportunities, the obvious needs in the American Church which were not at all well responded to, either by the diocesan structures or by the religious order structures. The first of them is the missed opportunities for the black Catholic community in the United States. There are honorable exceptions to that stricture of course, in some heroic instances on the part of individual diocesan priests or diocesan structures, but more often in the case of religious orders. What response there was to the need of the black community came mainly from such congregations as the Society of the Divine Word or the Society of St. Joseph in the cultivation of membership within their own ranks or in the foundation and operation of schools and seminaries.

Here too parishes in the black community were probably more often than not confided to religious orders.

The second missed opportunity was for the Hispanic Catholic community. In some ways it was like other ethnic communities. But more importantly, it was different in that it is part of our initial Catholic heritage, and it has, despite its millions of members, been all too "invisible" to most of us for all too long.

Third, often enough the institutionalization of original enterprises also involved, in Max Weber's terms, the "routinization of charisma." What had started out as a charismatic leadership enterprise in a particular apostolate, gathering enthusiastic participants into that apostolate, turned, as success followed success in the late nineteenth and early twentieth centuries, into some very routine work. Too often it was continued, one might have to say, simply because it had been begun.

Fourth, often enough regularity increasingly took precedence over adventure. Where bold initiatives had been undertaken in the beginning, as the religious orders grew, concern for the internal regularity of the order became paramount. An illustrative example is the case of the nineteenth century visitor to a particular religious order who encouraged the further entrance into the apostolate of education and the diminution of recruits for the apostolate of the Indian missions—not because the one was better than the other, but because, in his words, the community could be kept to greater spiritual regularity and internal domestic discipline in a school than it could on an Indian mission.

Finally, a caveat: A serious and sustained investigation of the history of the response of religious orders to the circumstances in which they found themselves in the United States would have to ask how much the apostolates undertaken by the religious orders were indeed a response to needs and how much simply a reaction to events.

IV. THE PRESENT AS THE LINK
BETWEEN PAST AND PROLOGUE

I have not wanted here simply to present historical data. Neither have I wanted to turn this material into a semi-disguised prophecy.

Rather, I would like to take the last ten years as linking years between the past and the future. What do they reveal about the accomplishments of the past that might serve as important background for what religious orders decide to do for the future? Of course those accomplishments have been ambivalent. They have been good or bad in all of their instances in theory, in interpretation and in action. "Long-range planning," as Peter Drucker says, "does not deal with future decisions but with the futurity of present decisions."

First, for the last two hundred years the religious orders in the United States neither carried on nor started out with their work in the presence of an elaborately and explicitly thought out theory of their apostolates in the United States. Rather, it has been a pragmatic response to apostolic needs. However, it seems to me that such an underlying theory did exist. It involved the inculturation of an immigrant Church, the preservation of the faith within the members of that Church, the increase of the Church through conversions, and an operative myth which embodied concepts of the nature of the Church, the nature of salvation and the nature of religious life together with particular practices which were either calculated to reinforce those concepts or seen as essentially flowing from them. When that theory of the apostolate and those concepts and the operative myth associated with it no longer worked, especially in the changing circumstances after Vatican II, a variety of dislocations resulted. We are still in the midst of those dislocations which have in some instances brought on chaos or at least anomie. The question might be asked, "Should we have such an explicitly thought out set of theories?" Some have tried to elaborate them in the last ten years. The question is still open whether they have functioned any better for the religious life than the non-explicitated theories of the past.

Next, the apostolates of the last two hundred years have often been begun by individual entrepreneurs. Often they have been continued by such individuals. In almost every case, however, those individuals had some kind of what I would call a strong "order identity." Those individuals were able to sustain their own personal work in the apostolate because of that identity with their congregations. What can we do to sustain such an "order identity"?

Third, those apostolates, no matter how individually started, were in many instances rapidly institutionalized, or made a corporate enterprise. When they were not so institutionalized, they very often faltered or produced far less results than might have been expected. An example here of non-corporativeness or non-institutionalization would be the work with prisons and prisoners, often done at great cost and heroic sacrifice by individuals but hardly ever taken on as institutional apostolates by an order or congregation. Another example would be the apostolate with the black Catholic community which has indeed been institutionalized in some instances. In almost every one in which it has been so institutionalized it has succeeded better than where it has simply been the work of individual members of an order or congregation.

Next, the commitments made to particular apostolates have most often been visibly seen. Sometimes those visible commitments have been seen as individual ones but also, and more importantly, they have often been seen as the corporate witness of orders or congregations as such. The question should be asked whether our apostolates for the future can be as successful as in the past if there is not some kind of continuing corporate community witness to them.

Fifth, often enough the institutionalization of a particular apostolate and the institutions themselves in which it was embodied came to be considered almost goods in themselves, which inhibited our freedom to move to new ventures. Perhaps the most obvious example here is the elaborate network of educational institutions which various orders undertook. Yet the ambivalence here, and it must be strongly emphasized, is that without such institutionalization, apostolates have been nowhere as effective as those so embodied in institutions.

Sixth, the religious congregations have shown an impressive capability of mobilizing their resources and dealing with realities or challenges that are presented in a simple and direct manner. An example of such a reality would be that of the appeal of the missions, or the salvation of souls, or the conversion of non-Catholics. The success of Maryknoll for the foreign missions and Glenmary for the home missions, both the men's and the women's congregations, provides impressive testimony of this. So far, however, the religious orders have been less capable of mobilizing such resources when it comes to dealing with more complex realities and more complex operative myths. For example, the question of the social order, of justice in society, of the social apostolate as a whole, has in general eluded the kind of organizational and institutional success which other apostolates have achieved. One of the reasons for this may be the lack of an operative myth compellingly attractive to the minds and hearts of members of religious congregations. Such myths are not manufactured overnight.

How they arise we ought to try to learn. To help them arise and take root we ought to bend all our efforts.

Lastly, just as the Church has been for a long time a cognitive minority—to use the term of the sociologist Peter Berger—so also congregations increasingly are a cognitive minority within the Church. By cognitive minority he would mean "a group of people whose view of the world differs significantly from the one generally taken for granted in their society." Such a group has to work at maintaining the credibility and the plausibility of its own belief structure in the face of all the various types of forces which tend to undermine it. Religious orders at the present time do say that they are an organized group of people, a community, whose view of the world does differ significantly often from the one generally taken for granted not only in the more general society but even from the one taken for granted within the membership of the Church. If religious communities are such, then internally they have to find the structures which will make life therein led plausible to its membership. Even more so, they will have to find ways of becoming signs of "meaning seeking." As Viktor Frankl has said in *Man's Search for Meaning*, "Most men and women seek, if not for themselves, at least some sign that there are others who have a sense of commitment which ideally would be final and irrevocable and to which those so committed would spend their lives in service." Such signs of commitment will no longer be visible simply through the rigid practices of the religious orders of the past. Such practices are in so many ways gone and they cannot, and in many ways fortunately will not, be called back. How then do we maintain such a sense of commitment internal to the orders while at the same time we engage in a variety of apostolates probably more varied and diversified than in the past while simultaneously we institutionalize them in order to preserve them for the future and in order to bring the best of our resources and strength to them for the present? That is for you as religious superiors and not for me as a historian to figure out and to decide. Again, as Peter Drucker has said, "Decision-making is *the specific* executive task." To do it creatively I think that we have to know our American Catholic heritage and reflect on it seriously. Then I think we have to go forward toward our mission with a vision.

CONCLUSION

Let me conclude by comparing two central myths or visions. Both of them in differing degrees are based on history and both of them are immensely powerful. Both of them you are well aware of. They are the stories of Odysseus or Ulysses and Abraham. They are not meant to provide answers; they are characteristic signs or signals, and one of them is also a great sign of hope.

Both of these stories are the stories of adventure and journeys. In the story of Odysseus in the *Odyssey* we have the journey of an individual or single man. That journey is portrayed all the way through as essentially a journey of return, a return to the familiar, a return to which the adventurer is driven because of nostalgia, which is simply a word derived from the two Greek terms for a pain or a longing for something which is known or familiar. Odysseus goes through an incredible series of adventures and journeys in order that he might finally come home to the familiarities of his wife Penelope and his son Telemachus—to his home, to his native land, even to his familiar hound dog.

The other story, that of Abraham, is the story indeed of an individual man, but he is never regarded simply as such. Rather he is a member of and the leader of a community. He is a man who, instead of returning to the familiar, is leaving the familiar—his familiar home in Ur of the Chaldees, and going from that home to a foreign land. He is sustained on a journey of hardship and uncertainty by the community of this family and brethren and by the conviction that he is called by God. It is the story of the journey of a man who lived on hope against hope in a faithful God who told him he would make his descendants as numerous as stars of the sky and the sands of the sea. It is the story of a man who had a hope in God whom we know now better than he knew him then.

Abraham was the heir of a past, and as such he had a heritage. We too are inevitably the heirs of our past. He also had a vision, and in that vision he served his God. We also have a heritage. We ought to get to know it better. We have a vision too, and in the strength of that vision we also are on a journey to a God who has said to us, quite simply, in the last book of Scripture, the Book of Revelation, "Behold, I make all things new."

HOPE-FILLED DEEDS
AND CRITICAL THOUGHT:
THE EXPERIENCE OF
AMERICAN MALE RELIGIOUS
AND THEIR NEED TO REFLECT ON IT

James Clifton, C.F.X.
John W. Padberg, S.J.
Jacques Pasquier, O.M.I.
Trini Sanchez, S.J.
David A. Fleming, S.M.

This paper was prepared for presentation to participants in the Third Inter-American Conference of Religious held at Montreal in 1977. It captures the mood and enunciates the mentality which was most characteristic of the Conference in the late 1970's.

Some readers will feel that the situation in religious life in the United States has already evolved considerably beyond what is described in this paper. At any rate, the paper highlights some key themes which will be further developed later in this volume.

The first section of the paper repeats some insights about the history of religious life in the United States drawn from Father Padberg's presentation of the previous year, and brings these insights to a greater level of generalizaton.

In general, "Hope-Filled Deeds and Critical Thought" is a good witness to the quickly evolving outlook of members of the Conference in the late 1970's.

The paper was prepared by a writing team composed of James Clifton, C.F.X., John Padberg, S.J., Jacques Pasquier, O.M.I., Trini Sanchez, S.J., and David Fleming, S.M. (editor).

I. THE PAST: A HISTORICAL VIGNETTE OF THE AMERICAN EXPERIENCE OF MALE RELIGIOUS

The history of religious life in the United States is riddled with apparent contradictions. Religious men in the United States throughout most of their history were noteworthy for combining "frontier deeds" with "base-camp thoughts." From the earliest days of colonization, through missionary work with native Americans, to the period of European immigration and consolidation, religious orders were involved in molding a new nation, often by means of bold deeds, while at the same time they preserved and handed on, with little reflection and almost no change, a theology and spirituality transplanted from European soil.

While protecting and nurturing the Christian lives of newcomers to the United States, religious men, clerical and lay, undertook to build institutions that would allow European Catholics to cope with the harsh demands of the frontier and the equally critical problems of large urban centers. Their work reveals a separatist, "siege," and "ghetto" mentality that saw at least some segments of American culture as threats to Catholic faith and morals. This mentality simply reinforced Catholic attitudes which in their European origins grew out of the Counter-Reformation and religio-political factors. Because this task of preservation was highly cherished by the American Catholic community at large, religious orders found acceptance and affirmation for their spiritualities and apostolates, as well as numerous American vocations.

At the same time the newness of the American experience was also having its effects. Separation of Church and state, a fundamental principle of the American Constitution from the beginning, evolved from a stance of hostile neutrality toward Catholicism to one of benign neutrality. In the face of this new historical experience, American Catholics, at first distrustful, gradually moved out of their timidity and were at pains to allay suspicion by protesting their patriotism and allegiance to the government, institutions, and ideals of the United States. They became noted for their fidelity (some would say their literal, uncritical acceptance) in regard to both papacy and flag.

The flourishing of male religious communities in the United States was greatly facilitated by the American tradition of reliance on voluntary institutions to meet the critical needs of society. In many lands almost every institution (with the possible exception of business corporations) owes its existence to a centralized state, is regarded as a creature of the state, and is subject in most details not to its own regulation but to regulation by the state. In contrast, we have the experience in the United States of voluntary institutions, associations, and organizations to meet most social, educational, cultural, and welfare needs. Examples range from the National Red Cross to regional academic accrediting associations to local ethnic cultural centers to religious groups such as the LCWR and the CMSM. The result is a system between *etatisme* (where the state regulates all) and anarchy.

This system curbed American individualism and allowed us to preserve a broadly shared confidence in the efficacy of institutions.

Religious orders were able to do "frontier deeds" in the American Church largely because they created and worked through such voluntary institutions and associations, for example, their schools and school systems. They multiplied the effectiveness of individuals over and over by working through such institutions. They were free to plan, institute, develop, change, or even disestablish such institutions because they were voluntary. No other country had quite this possibility to the same degree.

Yet religious orders largely failed to accompany their "frontier deeds" with critical reflection. They steadfastly held on to an ecclesiology, a spirituality, and sets of religious practices imported from Europe. Founders and their spirit were held in high regard, observances native and meaningful to another soil were scrupulously preserved, and even particular European nationalistic and cultural aspects of religious living were maintained, in forms of prayer, pious devotions, daily timetables, diet, and dress. American religious held on to these traditions while at the same time making externally major accommodations to a pluralistic and largely Protestant society and government.

Moreover, "active" religious institutes, in many cases founded under the influence of quasi-monastic, rural spirituality and strict observance, continued valiantly to preserve these, despite their increasing engagement in social ministries. This dichotomy and tension were accepted with little criticism or protest. Spiritual "exercises" were seen as marks of religious life, and as the power-base out of which apostolic activity received its vitality. But they also became open to mere routine and formalism in the hectic pace of the apostolate. Communal living meant living and sharing in common. Uniformity and identifiable externals, especially demeanor and dress, were taken for granted. Fidelity to and perseverance in one's vocation were highly valued within the religious community and in the larger Catholic community. An unreflective, legalistic interpretation of the evangelical counsels (consonant with the American preoccupation with law) found acceptance, especially after the promulgation of the new Code of Canon Law in 1918.

But while practices and observances tended to remain stable, the spirituality and values of American male religious were changing, sometimes quite unconsciously. In their praiseworthy efforts to minister to the Catholic population and at the same time to provide a secure place and better future for it, these religious uncritically tended to adopt many of the attitudes characteristic of the new nation. They were efficient, hard-working, activists, "doers," achievers, builders. They were loyal—to their communities, their faith and their country. They joined in the upward mobility of their fellow Catholics in the socio-economic order. Their institutions prospered and became models of success and stability. They themselves became constantly better educated, more widely recognized as "experts," "professionals." They became gradually and more clearly identified with the great American middle-class. And through all this development, they refused to compromise the spiritualities and observances they had inherited, much less critically examine them. And so the old continued to co-exist with the new. The dichotomies were accepted as part of one's vocation. The adjustments were hardly noticeable in the larger movement of American society. Questions or doubts were easily rationalized away.

II. THE PRESENT: SIGNS OF HOPE
AND SEEDS OF DEATH

The situation as described in the previous section prevailed almost universally until shortly before the Second Vatican Council. Since then it has altered drastically.

What is happening in religious life today reflects, without any doubt, some of the trends of the United States society. We would like briefly to underline some of the major shifts which are taking place in the United States.

After two hundred years, the spirit of building (the "frontier mentality") has disappeared. Economic recession, widespread unemployment, the energy crisis, the impact of the war in Vietnam, the trauma of Watergate—all have led American society to re-examine its values and question its own identity.

Are we a society passing from youth into "middle age," experiencing for the first time a "crisis of limits"? There is in our society a sense of disappointment, a lost hope manifest in pessimism and apathy. Suddenly, we are beginning to realize that we are no longer the society with "all the answers." We are questioning our own power. We wonder if our standard of living may have to be reduced. In our better moments, perhaps, we are moving to the stance of "pilgrims with questions."

Two crises seem particularly symptomatic and challenging for religious life:

1. the tendency to react to the dawning awareness of limits by protectionism, isolationism, privatism, and withdrawal—whether in the domain of foreign relations, international aid, and world trade, or in the private areas of dedication to social and charitable service;
2. the crisis of commitment, manifest in the breakdown of traditional values of family and marriage, in a hesitancy to make idealistic commitments ("Peace Corps," volunteer work in foreign countries) or permanent ones (religious life).

These crises are particularly disturbing in a society built on voluntary associations. If will power, courage, and private initiative are lacking, where will our society turn? And when you add these national crises to global upheaval and radical transformation in the Church, religious orders will obviously be affected in an acute way.

Yet signs of hope are abundantly present amid the signs of discouragement and death we have just been tracing. Ambivalence, more than anything else, characterizes congregations of religious men in the United States today. New images of the male religious, of his role and mission seem to be emerging, but they have not yet gained a consensus. The rapid rise in the average age of our membership and the continuing decline in our total numbers are sources of concern, but the flood of withdrawals has slowed considerably, and some encouraging signs of an increase in new vocations are present. In the following paragraphs, we aim to note some of the signs of hope and the seeds of death as we see them about us today.

Ministry

Despite the large-scale crisis just noted, religious orders of men in the United States today are more noteworthy for a growing sense of discomfort with the status quo and for a cautious measure of experimentation than for a sense of urgent and massive reorientation. The crises they have had to face since Vatican II have perhaps been experienced as somewhat less mammoth and devastating than those faced by other groups of religious in the Americas, largely because their ministries have not been so profoundly challenged by exterior circumstances (the castastrophic social problems of Latin America, the massive secularization of the Church in Quebec, the impact of the new consciousness of American women).

Yet significant changes are taking place. Religious orders of men in the United States are gradually giving greater emphasis to spiritual ministries (charismatic movement, spiritual direction, directed retreats) and social ministries (work for the poor, education toward justice). A more personalized sense of ministry seems to be developing, less dependent on structured roles within specifically Catholic institutions. Even within these institutions (which remain, for the most part, in the American tradition of "voluntary institutions"), new modes of presence are evolving in which religious communities aim very explicitly to Christianize the institution, to "animate" it, rather than simply to "staff" it. There is a lessening preoccupation with numbers, and a growing concern for quality and for the sharing of ministerial tasks beyond the institutional boundaries of the religious congregation.

The "declericalization of the Church" is having its effects. Many religious men are experiencing a broader ecclesial sense of ministry and a new emphasis on the full integration of religious women and lay persons as co-partners and full collaborators in the common mission. At the same time, many are confused by this "declericalization." The value of the religious life as such, as a witness and a radical commitment, apart from any clerical position and apart from any specific structured role, is not easily perceived. The result in identity crises, "drifting," depression, and withdrawal is evident for all to see.

Too many religious communities of men in the United States are still fearful to evaluate their institutional commitments; and in the face of declining and aging personnel, many of them cling uncritically to works which exhaust their manpower and crush hope of creativity. Such a lack of flexibility, if it continues, will be quite devastating in the decade ahead as the full impact of our recent lack of recruitment hits us.

Moreover, within the institutional commitments, the "demons of success" continue to tempt many religious to build their self-image and self-worth on their ability to produce and rise on a ladder of important positions, with a concomitant tendency to use even ethically questionable means (e.g., fund-raising gimmicks) in order to achieve success. When such temptations are not resisted, the sense of ministry wanes, and the inevitable "crisis of limits" experienced by all persons in late middle age becomes traumatic.

Prayer Life

The renewal of interest in and dedication to prayer is undoubtedly the most striking new phenomenon among American male religious in the past few years. This renewal of prayer life has touched the personal level in the form of an awakening interest in spiritual direction, directed retreats, and the development of new ministries in which spirituality is shared very directly with other religious and with lay people. More men are struggling to achieve a sense of integration in their lives with the help of regular reflection, spiritual direction, and seriously pursued personal programs of continuing formation. Participation in the charismatic movement has exerted a very powerful impact on a small number of men. Contemplative communities have become more anxious to share their own inner richness with active religious and some of them have become centers of prayer with a strong influence on those around them. In apostolic communities this renewal of prayer is most evident at the individual level. However, some communities are also beginning to evolve styles of common prayer which integrate spontaneity and structure and seem to offer a real promise of dynamic communitarian background for the life of union with God. There is a growth in shared prayer, dialogue homilies, and general ability and willingness to share faith both within religious communities and beyond them.

This universally welcomed renewal of the life of prayer calls for much more critical reflection than it has received so far. It is undoubtedly the result of a search for new roots now that the old, largely imported theologies and spiritualities are found wanting. Faddism plays a disturbing role in the search for a new spirituality. In some cases, this search probably tends to a privatist escapism in which social and ministerial concerns are left aside. Religious experience is perhaps too narrowly understood as simply a mystical communion with the Divine. There may be a danger of an over-emphasis on the specifically "spiritual ministries" (retreats, spiritual direction, houses of prayer, and the like). A false and inauthentic spirituality will develop if critical reflection does not lead us to integrate the new search for prayer with an equally strong and realistic search for service and for justice in the world. We are in danger of falling into an individualistic and therapeutic type of spirituality instead of a communitarian and service-oriented one. Perhaps too much of our spirituality is still colored by contrived "formational" experiences instead of by honest confrontation with the joys and sorrows, the pains and exaltations of real life.

Despite the paucity of critical reflection, however, there can be little doubt that the renewal of prayer and spirituality is the greatest sign of hope for American male religious today.

Community

Gradually we seem to be moving to the establishment of more open and human religious communities. The old paradigm of the community as a "barracks" from which soldiers of Christ might sally forth on their apostolic missions gave way shortly after Vatican II to the image of the religious community as a warm, receptive center in which each one might find boundless self-fulfillment. Both of these exaggerations now seem to be waning in favor of the movement toward an "evangelizing community," i.e., a community which listens to the word of God and man *as community,* shares and discerns the inspirations it receives, bears Christian witness in its life-style, attracts others to share in its life and mission, and then proclaims and serves as the word of God directs. The community is thus more clearly a communion of brothers in faith. Men living in community seem to feel a greater sense of personal freedom, while at the same time they are able more effectively to act in concert, sharing in the common discernment of God's will, in decision-making, and in the collegial exercise of authority. The younger religious, in particular, seem to have a more natural sense of such sharing and a less tense way of relating with religious superiors. Happiness and a high quality of life are more consciously accepted and legitimized as goals of religious community living. The pursuit of a community life style which bears some witness of simplicity seems to be widely accepted as a goal, although its implementation in real life still remains quite troublesome and spotty, and our middle class reflexes are still quite assertive. Religious as individuals and as communities are increasingly characterized by a more peaceful integration of sexuality, with a realistic sense of the need and possibility of intimate relationships compatible with the non-exclusive universal love expressed in the vow of chastity. All of these tendencies are only beginning; to say that the climate is improving on these issues is merely to say that a start has been made and that a period of extreme tension seems to have been replaced by one of gradual growth and integration.

At the same time, religious community life is in need of greater reflection. For many, community life remains a source of struggle and perplexity. On the part of a considerable number of men, we find an almost neurotic inability to change, manifest in conscious or unconscious sabotaging of any steps taken for community improvement. For some, the religious community seems to be too much a "nest" and source of security, an end rather than a means, a refuge than a springboard, a wall of separation rather than a stimulus to involvement. This security syndrome is especially alarming when it appears among entering candidates (some feel it is frequent among them). Among a certain number there is perhaps a distorted anxiety concerning the charism and individual identity of the congregation—an anxiety which channels an excessive amount of energy inward, blocks progress, and seeks to "turn back the clock" to recapture some imaginary ideal past. Moreover, religious communities are still plagued by a top-heavy age pyramid: most of them have a median age somewhere in the late forties or early fifties. In this situation, finances and the need for security in old age can become an excessive concern, determining too many administrative decisions and hampering new thrusts. Many groups tend to be reluctant to experience anything that is really new, placing an excessive degree of hope in the uncritical reappropriation, with slight retouching, of older forms of religious experience and community living. The individualism that seems characteristic of the American male remains a considerable problem.

It is apparently difficult for many religious to move from the extremes of passive dependence on the community and aggressive independence from it in favor of a sense of interdependence, in which each one can find his life enriched by the community and is in turn willing to give his gifts for its growth. Critical reflection is needed to give us the undergirding of a theology and a spirituality for meaningful and courageous community life.

The American Male Religious in the Context of the Whole Church

From the attitude of literal dependence on Europe and specifically on Rome which has characterized much of their history, many American male religious moved after the Second Vatican Council to the polar opposite of aggressive independence. Gradually, however, a breath of vision and an ecumenical and patient sense of pastoral development seems to be emerging. New ecclesiologies, based more on the sense of the "people of God," the "servant Church," and the "communion of believers" seem to be seeping explicitly or implicitly into our practical consciousness. There is better cooperation among religious communities and between religious and diocesan leadership. American male religious now seem to be better able to live within the institutional Church, to accept it without excesses of anger and impatience, while still taking challenging, perhaps prophetic stances. This attitude is evident in the calm though unfavorable response of many to recent curial pronouncements on sexual morality and the ordination of women.

The new ecclesiologies and the growing sense of interdependence are also evident in our relationships with Latin America and other countries of the third world. Even though many vestiges of the colonial outlook remain, it is clear that many American male religious in the third world are less attached to institutional permanence, more dedicated to the upbuilding of the indigenous Church, and readier to let go of their mentality and their positions of control. We still have a long way to go to catch up with current understandings of Church, but at least we have taken significant steps toward the conversion of our attitudes in overseas ministry.

On the negative side, a significant number of male religious show a loss of hope and a lack of vision regarding the Church and their role in it. It is clear to most of them that the old vision in which they were formed is decaying, but a new vision is not yet clear. The result too often tends to be an apathy or disenchantment with the institutional Church, leading to the individualistic tendency to build one's own "nest," and to a reluctance to take up any responsibility or any kind of clear prophetic role in relationship to the whole Church.

Moreover, the American male religious participates quite intensively in dichotomies between deed and thought which are of grave concern to the whole of American Catholicism, such as the dichotomy between theology and experience, the gulf between the academic and the pastoral, the general difficulty of critical reflection on the American experience, the difficulty of transcending ideologies (either "everything American is good" or "everything American is bad"), and a general lack of integration between one's Americanness, one's Catholicity, one's theology, one's religious charism, and one's personal commitment. This series of disintegrations could be quite dangerous in the long run for American Catholicism. We are best able to express the uniqueness of our American Catholic experience in terms of pluralism and pragmatism, but even these options seem to be immature and to cover over with words what is still an extremely problematic and cloudy reality.

III. OPTIONS AND IMAGES FOR THE FUTURE

The history of religious life has seen the rise of a succession of integrating images which have been the source of self-understanding, of theological reflection, of apostolic commitment, and of attractive power across the centuries. Thus the religious has been seen successively as "desert father," "monk in a large feudal monastic community," "mendicant friar," "counter-reformation soldier of Christ," and "anti-secularist institution builder." Each of these images has had its positive side and its day of overwhelming success in the history of the Church. Each has also had its "shadow side," with its excesses and containing seeds of decay which eventually led to periods of decline.

Today we seem to be passing into a new era, in which the future of religious life will depend upon the emergence of a new image which will be able to speak to the people of our time in the way that these former images spoke in the past. It is quite clear that the image of "anti-secularist institution-builder" has dominated during most of the history of religious life in the United States. Nearly all religious orders came to our country in a missionary effort to build institutions for immigrant communities. Even though there is a notable withdrawal from the "anti-institutional" stance that characterized young religious five years ago and even though we will undoubtedly continue to express our ministries through "voluntary institutions" in the American style, it seems clear that the role as "institution-builder" is no longer adequate as a comprehensive option of the American male religious for the future.

In the face of the inadequacy of this traditional model and image of religious life, many alternative models and images are frequently and passionately under discussion. Among them, the following seem to be predominant:

1. *The prophetic option:* According to this model, the religious would stand as a sign of contradiction, dialectically confronting contemporary life with the searing light of revelation and announcing his faith-insights regardless of the consequences. His vowed freedom would allow him to be prophetic, affirming the divine call and denouncing prevalent pseudo-values in opposition to it. From this prophetic stance would emerge a clear commitment to social justice, to the development of freedom, a real sense of the responsibility of the United States before the rest of the world, and a sense of the radicality of the Gospel. Although prophetic activity is certainly conceivable in institutional and communitarian contexts, proponents of the prophetic option naturally tend to give low priority to these contexts in their scenario for the future of religious life. The prophetic stance is generally understood as involving great freedom from institutional commitments and an ongoing, constant, and hopefully productive tension with the hierarchical element of the Church.

2. *Religious life as Gospel community:* This model sees the religious as one who throws in his lot with a group of people who together (a) listen to the word of God, hear the cry of their fellow man, and reflect in common on its significance, (b) evolve a life-style which witnesses to the values they have discerned in the process of listening, (c) proclaim this message to all those about them, (d) attract others to share in their discernment, their witnessing, and their mission, and (e) then enter into service of all manner and kinds, whether within specifically Catholic institutions or beyond them. The resultant model of the evangelizing coummunity tends to see the community as a whole as bearer of the mission and apostolic commitment, rather than each individual alone. The "evangelizing community" image is one which, like that of the "institution-builder," can integrate a variety of talents, ages, and perspectives into a common view. On the other hand, it presents a difficult challenge to the personalism and emphasis on individual charisms evident in the American Church today.

3. *Witness to freedom:* The thrust of this model is to channel the energies of individuals and communities not in the direction of the observance of prefabricated norms but rather into living the freedom of the Gospel as it appears in a constantly evolving life-process. The vows are not to be defined abstractly, but experientially. A religious community is always to be in process, determining what structures and what commitments will best explicate its Gospel dedication in a given situation. The boundaries between religious communities and dedicated lay people may become less clear, and religious "communions" may arise in which those dedicated to poverty, celibacy, and obedience in some traditional sense would mingle freely with those who do not have these dedications. The aim is not lawlessness and total lack of structure but rather a constant freedom and challenge to structure one's life in accord with the demand of God's call at a given time.

4. *Commitment to diakonia:* This model sees the religious as a person who lives Christian faith in a very explicit option for the poor, the oppressed, and all those who fall into the scriptural category of the anawim. Some would describe religious communities as "servant communities" whose whole thrust of existence is that of finding the best way to serve those who are marginalized by society as a whole. Although this group is not anti-institutional in principle, it is often highly critical of our present institutional commitments, judging that they are excessively devoted to "saving the saved" and not reaching out sufficiently to those in greatest need. Others would rather insist on an individual servant role and feel that community and institutional aspects would not be intrinsic to the living out of diakonia in religious life.

5. *Option for theoria:* This option sees the religious person as one dedicated to thought, reflection, and contemplation in the broadest sense of the term. Religious, like intellectuals and artists in civil society, try to attain and express a deeper understanding and a vision of the world about them. For religious the vision specifically focuses on God's action in the world and man's response to that action. The role of the religious, in this option, is to explicate a contemporary Christian vision and call other Christians to action in tune with the insights which result from their study, reflection, and prayer.

It is evident that all five of these options and images are exercises in creative imagination. Each of them has its strengths and its weaknesses. The judgmental urgency of the "prophet-religious" may lead to an attitude of elitism. The united thrust of the "evangelizing community" can degenerate into in-breeding and the stifling of individuality, and can discourage self-criticism, courage and risk. The "religious as thinker" may become elitist and far removed from the realities of daily life; the member of the "community dedicated to Christian freedom" may lose identity and become indifferent to the institutional Church. The "servant-religious" may lack spiritual depth and become excessively and violently involved in the intricate by-paths of worldly power. No vision is without its dangers.

However, it is evident that the five options just articulated are not totally exclusive. They all have in common a great emphasis on reflection, listening to the word of God, discernment and a depth of spirituality; all of them insist on free and alert response to the signs of the times, and on explicit proclamation and witness. In regard to community, these images offer a spectrum of possibilities: from the purely "apostolic group," whose primary gaze is outward and looks to community life only as a necessary support for its work, to the "monastic community" which finds its first reference point in its inner religious life and only looks secondarily to whatever kind of outreach flows from the group. Different options are valid among these images of the future, and these different options will lead to different emphases and different forms of richness.

This is why, as a conclusion to this paper, we would like to suggest interdependent diversity as our preferred option for the future of religious life.

We believe in a healthy diversity among religious congregations and even within them. The Church is still in a period of rapid development, and we do not believe that the time is ripe for a definitive fixing of the forms and emphases of religious life. On the practical level, we are still engaged in many creative experiments whose results can only be evaluated on a long-range basis. On the level of thought, we feel ourselves to be in the midst of a fruitful and challenging rethinking of our theologies, our spiritualities, our ecclesiologies, and our ministries. Society as a whole is opening up beyond the bounds of our Western world, both in its life-styles and in its modes of reflection. All of this ferment promises to enrich and deepen religious life in the long run, if we have the faith and patience to live with considerable ambiguity.

Yet we believe that the constantly burgeoning diversity of the foreseeable future must be interdependent. If contemporary experience is teaching us anything, it is a lesson about our global unity, our mutuality, our need for one another. There is no way for the Church in any one part of the world, still less for any one religious congregation, to pick a clear and neatly defined model for its internal use and then act independently of the rest of the Church and world that surrounds it. At least there is no way for this process to be a creative and enriching one. Each religious congregation will be unique in its particular style because of its distinctive history, structure, spirit and ministry; yet each must be oriented to increasing interaction with the rest of the Church and with all persons of good will in order to make a contribution at their side to the needs of a suffering world and to the upbuilding of God's kingdom.

Within this context of interdependent diversity, certain common elements will and should characterize all religious congregations in the future. These common elements may be synthesized in the phrase: communities of prophetic service.

The human race today is characterized by a longing and searching for *community,* motivated in part by the decay of former self-understood forms of community such as the patriarchal family, the rural parish, and the village. In response, religious congregations are being called to bear intensified witness to the "one mind and one heart" of Gospel living and to the Christian sisterhood and brotherhood which responds to some of humanity's deepest spiritual yearnings in our time. Some religious groups will continue to stress a community of life shared in daily proximity under a single roof. Others will evolve new forms of community that offer a tangible sense of belonging and a depth of support even though the members may be widely scattered for the sake of mission. All religious communities which survive in the future, however, will be known for their strong, existential, not merely juridical, sense of shared life and shared faith.

Religious congregations of all traditions, from the most "monastic" to the most "active," will continue to be devoted to service. The forms of ministry and the methods of caring will continue to evolve and flexible structures will be developed to channel this thrust for service, often into the "voluntary institutions" that are typical of American society. But whatever the forms and structures, dedication in charity to meeting the needs of the Church and the world will remain a constitutive hallmark of all forms of religious life.

Finally, religious communities that live on into the future will have to develop more fully their "prophetic consciousness." Their style of life and their forms of service will have to be a challenge and a witness, not merely an unreflective support for American secular culture. The vows are prophetic in themselves, bearing witness to the presence of grace where it is often hidden in ordinary life. But in addition, religious communities are gradually learning and must continue to learn not to be simply acquiescent in the "business as usual" of American culture. They will have to learn to speak a prophetic word more clearly, more effectively, more prayerfully, to a society enmeshed in self-interest and hedonism, to a government overwhelmed by its own power, and to the Church itself.

"Communities of prophetic service" such as these will continue to cultivate a life of prayer, will continue to seek the fullness of the Gospel through some commitment to evangelical counsels, and will continue to dedicate themselves to ministry. But all these elements must be allowed to develop still further in a context of faith-centered and hope-filled interdependent diversity.

THE ROLE OF U.S. RELIGIOUS
IN HUMAN PROMOTION

Barbara Kraemer, O.S.F.
Phil Land, S.J.
Joan Puls, O.S.F.

An ever-deepening involvement in the commitment of today's Church to issues of justice and peace is evident throughout this volume. Emerging gradually
through the 1970's, the consciousness of justice and peace issues among men religious was highlighted in the Statement of Goals adopted by the National Board
of the CMSM in 1979, which spoke of the call of religious "to a prophetic stance
in solidarity with all of God's people" and expressed a commitment "to promote
and be spokespersons for justice and human rights."

The 1980 Vatican document entitled "Religious and Human Promotion,"
published jointly with a companion document on "The Contemplative Dimension
of Religious Life," led to the development of the thrust toward justice and peace
and to reflection on it. These documents were preceded by an extensive consultation of religious throughout the world, including members of the Conference
of Major Superiors of Men. After the publication of the documents, representatives of the men and women religious leadership conferences of the United
States joined with their counterparts from the Canadian Religious Conference
and the Conference of Latin American Religious to review the documents and
coordinate efforts for work at the promotion of justice and peace.

Written as part of the reflection process following the publication of the Vatican documents, the following study was prepared as a joint project of the CMSM
and the Leadership Conference of Women Religious. Its authors are Barbara
Kraemer, O.S.F., Phil Land, S.J. and Joan Puls, O.S.F.

This paper is a reflection on the role that religious in the United States
play in human promotion. It identifies the context in which religious
discern their role, questions that they struggle to answer, and responses that they are making to the urgent social and political crises
of our times.

This reflection is prompted by the study of two documents of the
Sacred Congregation for Religious and Secular Institutes, printed in
1980: *Religious and Human Promotion* and *The Contemplative Dimension of Religious Life*.

SOCIO-ECONOMIC AND POLITICAL CONTEXT

It is extremely important to situate the role and response of religious within the current framework of U.S. socio-economics and U.S. politics.

In a general analysis, the United States is and has been an economic military superpower. Defining itself as a bastion of freedom and democracy for the world, the United States has espoused a foreign policy since World War II of reaction to the Soviet Union and to a perceived Communist threat around the globe. Unsure of itself since the Vietnam experience, the United States clamors to demonstrate once again its primacy.

The United States is essentially a free and open society. It believes itself to be the most benevolent country in the world (witness the Marshall Plan and the foreign aid record). U.S. society is largely middle-class, and, until recently, a society of rising expectations. There are, however, significant numbers of both rich and poor. Economic crises in the United States in recent years have both produced misery for our own poor and have resulted in a waning concern for the pressing problems of third and fourth world countries.

If current trends prevail, the immediate future will be characterized by more of the following:

- a decreased concern for the protection and development of human rights and dignity, both at home and throughout the world;
- a new emphasis on free market philosophy, on rewarding our allies and punishing those peoples who fail to lend support;
- a new emphasis on the Communist threat, prompting arms-buildup (at the expense of social programs), nuclear weapons, a neglect of the North/South issues;
- a de-emphasis on government's role in protecting the quality of life: air, water, regulation of land use, use of the oceans;
- an impetus for churches to engage in uncharacteristic public debate over issues: policies regarding Latin America, abortion, tuition tax credit, taxation of religious personnel and institutions, arms limitations, social welfare, plight of refugees, death penalty, etc.

CULTURAL IMPACT

U.S. culture has a significant impact on the approach of U.S. religious to their role in human promotion. This paper cannot explore that culture exhaustively, but will present one aspect, the political, that affects the role of U.S. religious.

For decades, the Church has emphasized the distinction between the sacred and the secular, between the realm of the spiritual and that of the temporal. It was inevitable that many religious would accept that distinction and live out its implications. For example, certain issues are reserved for the professional politician or for extra-curricular involvement. Many people would support a mission collection or endorse a contribution to a Catholic college or seminary, while not finding any religious motive for opposing the draft, for protesting cuts in social programs, or for withholding tax money that is directed to weapons buildup.

One exception to this dichotomy in recent years has been political action taken on behalf of a pro-life stance. And there are other hopeful signs of change. Increasingly, bishops and others in the Church are encouraging their co-Christians to enlarge the arena in which they integrate their moral values with their rights and duties as citizens. Hence we now witness public positions of Church men and women regarding nuclear disarmament, the death penalty, and the protection of human rights in Latin America.

Insofar as the spirit of Vatican II has taken hold, there is a rethinking of this integrated approach to the needs of the times. Still, the spiritual formation of religious leaves much to be desired by way of preparing them for carrying out the mandates of Vatican II in daily life and in the marketplace. Many still lack a global vision of the issues of poverty, the arms race, ecology, forms of oppression. Many still do not recognize or engage in ecumenical efforts on behalf of justice. Many are unwilling to participate in the process of legislative change. While there is a growing consciousness of solidarity with the poor, there is not enough of a sense of the role of the poor in *our* evangelization. Many *believe in* mutuality in our relationship with the poor, but they do not place themselves where they *experience* it.

A second thread in this religious culture strengthening the separation of the religious from the world is the Church's reaction to the Enlightenment. As the churches (Protestant as well as Catholic, throughout Europe as well as in the United States) saw the Enlightenment enthrone reason and science while degrading religion and the sacred sciences, their mistaken reaction was to abandon the secular in favor of a ghetto of the sacral, hoping to be kept free from any contamination with the secular. The disastrous separation carried on for decades, and only Vatican II produced a clear theology that encouraged Catholics once again to believe they are missioned to this world.

A third factor in this cultural orientation applies more uniquely to the United States. This is the separation of Church and state in tradition and in Constitution. The creators of the U.S. Constitution wanted no more of the tyranny of established religions. In itself this had some good effects. One example: freed from direct link to the state, religious were free to critique political structures and policies in the light of the Gospels. But in the main, the separation of Church and state reinforced dualism and a negative reaction to the Enlightenment. Church-oriented people drew the unfortunate conclusion that the political order was not for them.

This was only too evident in the Church's educational system. The schools (and public education is included here) did little to prepare for the life of the *polis*. Many failed to base their attitude toward social issues on a developed philosophy of responsibility for the common good. In failing to prepare us for a Christian approach to politics, our educational system contributed to making religious as well as lay people victims of implicit ideologies, such as the American Dream. "More is better" was often a guiding principle rather than "sparing and sharing" or a "theology of enough." There was little encouragement to be critical, to be counter-cultural in the spirit of the Gospel. As a result, religious and laity absorbed ideologies unreflectively, so that their decisions in politics often stemmed from premises *inconsonant* with the Gospel.

These failures were pointed out by the 1971 Synod of Bishops in their document *Justice in the World*. Special reference is made to the impact of narrow individualism, materialism, the pseudo-values inculcated by the communications media and the negative consequences these have upon Christian conscience and Christian practice. "Education demands a renewal of heart, a renewal based on the recognition of sin in its individual and social manifestations."

The same document makes clear that social and religious activity can never be fully separated. Christians, lay and religious, have the right and duty to promote the common good, acting under the influence of the Gospel and the teaching of the Church. Such temporal obligations as voting are to be fulfilled with fidelity and competence. Since party politics are not noticeably ideological in the United States it is particularly incumbent upon Christians to examine candidates and issues carefully, in the light of their total impact upon society. It is not enough to take a narrow position based upon one issue and neglect the total range of issues affecting human promotion. Religious must maintain a special awareness of the deeper implications of their political activity and leadership in the political arena.

The preceding points lead to some pertinent questions for U.S. religious:

1. How can we join others in calling the U.S. Catholic Church, in all of its institutional manifestations (dioceses, parishes, educational and health-care institutions, our own religious communities, national organizations such as the National Council of Catholic Bishops, the Leadership Conference of Women Religious, the Conference of Major Superiors of Men), away from excessive concern with its own life to a greater emphasis on bringing about the reign of God on earth?

2. How can we use the prevailing situation of separation of Church and state as a guarantee of the Church's prophetic role and not allow it to limit the areas of Church action?

3. How can we encourage one another to be prophetic, accepting the attendant risk of being misunderstood by various groups in Church and society?

4. How can we expand the agenda of church groups to include *all* critical and moral issues facing U.S. society and the rest of the world?

5. How can we better appreciate the complexity of the questions faced by lay men and women (e.g., loss of a job or acceptance of moral responsibility) and cooperate with them in finding Christian resolutions?

THE CHALLENGE FACING U.S. RELIGIOUS

Contemporary religious, alive to the Spirit and sensitive to the plight of their brothers and sisters, cannot ignore the pressing implications of the current political scene. More and more they realize their responsibility to speak and act regarding some of the blatant and unjust political policies of this decade. More and more religious refuse to sit silently or remain indifferent in the face of increased military spending, proposed missile systems, new nuclear submarines, neutron bombs, and the U.S. role as arms producer for much of the world.

Religious see their specific ministries, their opportunities as educators, their influential roles as pastors and leaders, as calls to speak against various forms of discrimination: against minorities, homosexuals, women, the disabled, the poor. Religious, as they deepen their identity with the values and life-style of Jesus, find ways to express concern for undocumented aliens, the unborn, battered women, political prisoners, Latin American peasants. Some are called to speak on their behalf and to empower others to speak for themselves.

Religious today are more aware of the necessity of combining short-range projects of feeding the hungry and healing the sick with long-range efforts to insure just structures and to humanize social systems. They are coming to realize the connections between our U.S. life-style and issues affecting our environment and our use of energy, and issues that affect the poor and the powerless. They are called to a greater sharing of resources and to a style of living that takes into account its effects on others.

As Christians and as religious, we have *prayed* over our reflections and our responsibility to recognize the plight of other human beings. Our prayer is ineffective without personal and political action to effect structural change, and to encourage interdependence. We are called to devise and practice a pedagogy for ourselves, the middle class, the non-poor, and to put flesh on a theology of *letting go*. We are challenged to reorient our life and ministry with the poor, so that we mutually receive from and learn from one another.

Religious actively involved in facing these issues sometimes find that Church definitions of their role in the political realm leave them with unanswered questions. Must not religious, they ask, be involved in the politics of change, from injustice to justice? Isn't the way of

Jesus our way? And wasn't his way one of publicly witnessing, denouncing, announcing? If he were present today . . .

Religious who are concerned with justice have come to realize that injustices are imbedded in social and economic structures and that these constitute social sin. Abuse of power underlies these sinful structures. How desensitized we in the United States, e.g., have become to the social sins of violence and racism. Religious are led to realize that an authentic witness requires speaking out against social sin.

Further and continuing questions face religious:

1. How can we best combine our justice and charity ministries, working with and for the poor and learning from them, together using our experience to deepen our understanding of social issues?

2. How can we best minister to middle class members of the U.S. Catholic Church in the face of a growing need to be a prophetic Church?

3. How can we live in solidarity with the poor and minorities of the United States and the world, given the strengths and weaknesses of our middle class character?

4. How can we promote justice *within* the Church, that it may be a more credible sign of justice to others?

5. What examination must we make of our life-style (personally, corporately, institutionally) if we are to be credible witnesses?

RESPONSES OF U.S. RELIGIOUS

Increasingly in recent years and with the encouragement of Church documents, U.S. religious have been seriously examining their role in contemporary life. Whether it be an examination of the social implications of the vows, an assessment of life-style, a concern for the integration of contemplation and action, or the corporate responsibility of religious trying to effect change in the social order, religious are struggling to be obedient to the call of the Gospel and the

Church. In revising their constitutions, in community renewal programs, in evaluation of their ministry, religious are dialoguing, reflecting, risking, to be more evident signs of Jesus' life and values. The struggle is not smooth and the tension that arises is not easily resolved. However, slowly and with discernment, religious communities are finding ways to renew their personal ideals, to find a rhythm of prayer/solitude and service of others, and hopefully to give a united witness to their hope for the coming of the reign of God.

Many religious have chosen to minister in less-traditional approaches to education and health care. More religious are working with others, religious and lay, in Catholic Worker houses, prisons, women's shelters, campus ministry, retreat direction, drug and alcohol clinics, community health centers, farm worker and migrant ministry. Many religious are ministering in works of social service as new forms of presence within civic and private organizations. Women religious have grown increasingly conscious that they have much to share with and to learn from other women. Ministries are seen more in terms of their relationship to issues of justice and in terms of global awareness. New ministries are being born with a view to the building of *community*, locally, and the building of *networks*, nationally and internationally.

U.S. religious are also learning from people of other cultures. Responding to the invitation to read the signs of the times, religious discover that the most eminent sign is the groanings of the oppressed and that the suffering faces of these oppressed reflect the anguished face of Christ in their midst, calling all in the Church to join them in their struggles. The call of Popes, synods, episcopal conferences like Puebla, to a preferential option for the poor means concretely an identification with the struggle of the poor to change the structures that prevent them from achieving a full human life for themselves and their families.

Effects of the influence of other cultures and other groups are manifested in the beginning of basic Christian communities in the United States, in ecumenical work for justice, in coalitions for peace and solidarity, in prophetic actions, in witness in daily life.

Based on their experience, reflection, and confidence in the mission entrusted to them, religious have found the following responses to be legitimate and necessary:

1. *Denouncing injustices and dissenting:* Earlier sections list a number of ways in which religious believe our own government and people (and Church, not to say our own congregations) are guilty of injustices. These injustices must be denounced. Everywhere we witness the intolerably excessive share that the rich and powerful are able to shift to themselves, depriving the poor and weak of the benefits of properly ordered government. Returning missionaries have made U.S. religious more conscious of the extent to which governments of our mission-sending countries may be exploiters. Religious are coming to see better that we are part of the problem of the poor nations, another cogent reason for religious playing active roles.

2. *Educating and conscientizing:* Religious carry out much of the educational work of the Church through schools and other ministries of continuing education. If our education is to be a renewal based on the recognition of individual and social sin, then we have awesome "political" responsibilities:

   - to arouse a consciousness of the forces of injustice;
   - to develop a critical sense with respect to values in society;
   - to present a global context to the life of individuals and communities.

Such education, though encouraged by the social teaching of the Church, will be considered subversive by many.

3. *Announcing: The Call to Action (Octogesima Adveniens)* invites all in the Church to exercise that vision which reaches beyond all existing forms of society and, in the light of the Gospel, imagines a new earth. We are to be creating this new earth now. Those opposing the engagement of religious in "political" education will equally reject their searching for a new society, that is to say, for the religious values that ought to impregnate such a renewal of society. Religious announce the reign of God when they are willing to speak and give witness to their beliefs.

4. *Taking sides with the poor and oppressed:* Religious, in giving active support to the struggles of the poor and oppressed, believe they are

only heeding the call of the recent Popes, of Paul VI in his *Evangelica Testificatio,* of John Paul II in his recent encyclicals and in numerous other talks. U.S. religious are also familiar with the same call emerging from Medellín and Puebla (the Latin American Bishops' Conferences of 1968 and 1979). Consequently, religious believe that if they are to have any true sign value, they must be in the midst of the poor and oppressed and be supporting the liberation and humanization of people. A number of activities in this respect are widely practiced by U.S. religious. Among these are:

- giving talks and providing community education on issues;
- supporting and lobbying for reform legislation, such as less regressive taxation, increased health benefits for the poor, unemployment aid;
- signing letters of protest;
- marching in favor of the exploited;
- taking firm stands against forms of racism;
- holding liturgies and prayer vigils of protest;
- creating communities of witness and service.

5. *Denouncing abuses by multinational corporations through stockholders' suits:* U.S. religious have discovered and refined a creative tool for reaching the consciences of corporate executives and boards of trustees of large corporations. They initiate formal motions for disclosure of certain immoral or oppressive practices of such international corporations and present motions with requisite signatures at small stockholders' meetings. The result has been a raising of consciousness both of the corporations and of a wider public. Their action has been of some consequence in the disputes regarding infant formula and others.

6. *Guiding movements:* Some religious have played important roles in helping to guide trade unions, workers' movements, family centers, community health centers, etc., into channels supportive of the preceding lines of activity and away from a traditional emphasis on exclusively individual goals.

7. *Creating communities:* U.S. religious view with sympathy the work of religious in Latin America, in particular their role in commu-

nity-building. Such new communities, where they grow in strength and take on a sense of direction, become a new political force—perhaps the only truly people's movement available in situations of oppression. Some counterparts to these are peace communities, alternate life-style groups, and coalitions for justice, in all of which the laity play prominent roles.

8. *Assuming leadership roles:* With growing experience, religious in the United States have been able to undertake certain forms of direct political activity. They vote. They endorse candidates who stand for justice. A few religious have run for office in the hope of effecting change, or, at least, of giving witness to specific Gospel concerns and values. Above all, U.S. religious support the laity in their exercise of political leadership.

9. *Accepting a prophetic role:* U.S. religious congregations have in general been prepared to accept in varying degrees what has come to be called prophetic action. This may take the form of *extra*-legal, *para*-legal, or even illegal action. One example: denouncing, through civil disobedience, the Vietnam War and, more recently, the continued arms race. Another: participating in strikes. Apropos of this latter example and also of several political actions already mentioned, religious often feel that staying out of the fray leaves the laity, who have many responsibilities religious do not have, alone to bear the brunt of the struggle for justice.

THEOLOGICAL BASIS

Surely Vatican II was revolutionary in placing the Church *in* the world, as a penetrating rather than a parallel presence. *Gaudium et Spes,* after asserting that governing the world with justice and holiness is the Creator's will, concludes that people "can justly consider that by their labor they are unfolding the Creator's work . . . and contributing to the realization in history of the divine plan" (n. 34; cf. also nn. 38, 39, 57).

It is not alongside this history of humankind that the reign of God is revealed, but within it. And it is within the same history that we participate in the coming of that reign. Our work in support of justice for and with our neighbor, insofar as it is obedience to God's absolute command of love of neighbor, is an expression of our love of God. So long as it is genuine love of our neighbors that brings us to support their process of humanization, it is of eternal validity and meaning.

If God's reign is embodied here and now in human history, then salvation takes place in history. For the two histories—sacred and secular—do not run side by side, but the former within the latter. This has profound meaning for religious. They cannot be denied an active role in the here and now of God's reign, in their political reality, in the political dimension of love of neighbor.

Jesus loved his humanity and progressively showed his humanness, a process that culminated in his dying. Jesus loved that humanity he shared with us, and loves its progressive improvement as embodiment of the reign of God. Religious, consequently, find it necessary to be engaged directly in the liberation and humanization of their people.

These theological reflections, which thrust the Church and the Christian deep into the humanization of life, have consequences for the collaboration in mission of religious and laity. Religious have often questioned why some Church authorities neatly attribute to the laity the realm of the secular and to the religious that of the sacred. Religious experience solidarity with the laity in demonstrations for nuclear disarmament, in prayer vigils for the oppressed of El Salvador, in communication with members of Congress to stop military support of repressive regimes.

Two theological considerations seem to support a more intimate collaboration of laity and religious. First is the fact that the mission to evangelize and to work for the reign of God is given to both laity and religious by their common baptism.

This acceptance of a common mission is strengthened by *Lumen Gentium*'s symbol of Church as "people of God." If all are people of God, do we not have a common task to be achieved jointly? Other Christian communities reflect this intimacy and unity of acting for a common mission. And this is the direction that basic communities are taking.

The distinction is often quoted, from *Gaudium et Spes* (n. 42), that the Church has no proper mission to the secular but that its role is religious. One can understand this in a correct light as saying that the Church brings to secular history the light of the Gospel and the grace and fellowship of Jesus Christ and the Holy Spirit. But the danger in the expression is that it is often taken to mean that secular history is one world and religious history another. As mentioned earlier, this was the reaction of the Catholic Church to the Enlightenment, with the tragic result that Christians left this world to the devil (i.e., the Enlightenment). Proper autonomy and distinction of roles, called for by *Gaudium et Spes,* can be safeguarded even while calling upon the Church to play a vigorous role in secular history.

A theology of the Church in the world has relevance for spirituality. There have been notable advances in theology of spirituality since Vatican II. Two factors have contributed immensely. The first is more reliance on *experience.* It is not that charisms or authoritative pronouncements are held invalid. It is only that religious have learned from the Council to read the signs of the times. They understand what significance the aspirations of peoples, the movements of our times, specific events, have for the coming of God's reign. Scripture and documents such as *Justice in the World* have helped religious to reflect on where people are, what their needs are, and what that has to say about how they as religious live and pray and act.

Whereas religious life was once viewed as a closed community of the vowed, it is now more readily seen as an intensified form of announcing God's reign, through public witness. There is no rejection of the witness that in an earlier day was the hallmark of the religious life. But there is a new insistence that authentic witness must be *incarnational* (thereby avoiding excessive stress on the transcendental and the loss of contact with people and their real needs).

In searching for the incarnational, spirituality widely became expressed in terms of mission. *Gaudium et Spes* expressed that mission as the humanization of life. The 1971 Synod, in *Justice in the World,* narrowed that mission more specifically to justice and liberation (as did also *Evangelii Nuntiandi*). The bishops at Puebla and John Paul II (but many religious congregations well in anticipation) focused still more sharply that mission of justice and liberation on the needs of the poor and called for a preferential option for the poor. Within this mission, the mission to and with the poor, religious are called to witness, give service, pray and reflect, renew their life-style. They are called to encounter Jesus in people seeking humanization, liberation, and an end to crippling poverty. They are called, above all, to new faith and new commitment, as they are evangelized *by* the poor.

It is generally the belief of religious that in this mission they encounter most powerfully the paschal mysteries. The cross itself takes on for them a new dimension. The crucified Jesus went to his death because he dared to liberate from sin and death, from those powers and principalities embedded in unjust structures, from burdensome interpretations of the Torah, from a priesthood that bound people in darkness. Christ identified with the poor and powerless in his day. And this it was that brought him to his death on the cross.

It is in the mystery of the incarnation that God comes to us. And it is only in and through our humanity that we go to God. Further, in the paschal mysteries of death, resurrection and glorification, Jesus takes on as an extension of himself the body of the world. It is very much in and through that extension of the Lord, which is his body, that we meet God. The human family must be viewed in some real sense as the body of Christ.

Christian spirituality, therefore, must be rooted in experience and in our identification with the body of Christ. It must be integrated. Through reflection and interiority, we are opened and made sensitive to the action and the word of God. Prayer needs and sustains community. Simplicity and justice need and sustain prayer and community. Contemplation makes us aware of the power of God working in our life and in the world around us, and empowers us to respond to that movement. As our faith in the process of God's reign grows, our life is radically changed. We become persons for others, builders of community, constantly renewed by prayer and communal discernment. We move into human life and ministry with a greater depth of understanding and compassion.

SUMMARY

Congregation after congregation of religious have declared in assemblies and chapters a willingness and a need to identify with the poor, to witness solidarity with the victims of injustice, to serve them, to empower them, to be brought to faith and courage by them, to enter together into the struggle for global justice, precisely as an exercise of faith and commitment as religious.

Increasingly the stance of religious constitutes a prophetic word spoken to the world and to its political reality. If this word is to be a word that hastens the reign of God, it must have first of all transformed those who speak it. The task of religious is to be faithful to the demands of the Gospel, to be so radically influenced by it that they can embody it in their history.

PILGRIMS AND PROPHETS: SOME PERSPECTIVES ON RELIGIOUS LIFE IN THE UNITED STATES TODAY

David A. Fleming, S.M.
Robert Berson
Wilfrid Dewan, C.S.P.
Virgil Elizondo
Lawrence Madden, S.J.
Ronald Pasquariello, F.M.S.

The Inter-American Conferences of Religious have been especially significant in promoting the development of reflection during recent years in U.S. religious life. "Pilgrims and Prophets" was the contribution of the Conference of Major Superiors of Men to the Fourth Inter-American Conference held at Santiago, Chile in November 1980.

"Pilgrims and Prophets" repeats themes found elsewhere in this book but also manifests a significant development in thought and a greater clarity in direction on the part of the Conference. This paper continues to be used, probably more than any other single document, as a guideline for the life of the Conference up to the present time.

The paper was drafted by the Religious Life and Ministry Committee of the CMSM, which at the time consisted of David A. Fleming, S.M. (Chairperson); Robert Berson, Glenmary; Wilfrid Dewan, C.S.P.; Virgil Elizondo; Lawrence Madden, S.J.; and Ronald Pasquariello, F.M.S. The paper was submitted to an extensive consultation process in the regional meetings of the Conference and at the Annual Assembly of 1980. A representative sampling of bishops, women religious, and lay leaders were also consulted. The paper was finalized by the Religious Life and Ministry Committee and edited by David A. Fleming, S.M.

During the past several years, the Conference of Major Superiors of Men of the United States (CMSM) has been involved in a process of reflection on goals and priorities. In our tasks as congregational leaders, we are increasingly moved by new perceptions of the Church and our role in it. These perceptions, still nascent, seem strange to some of our members. Yet, despite lingering uncertainty and vagueness, we find ourselves using certain words with greater frequency and growing conviction—words such as pilgrimage, prophecy, solidarity, communion, freedom, contemplation.

This paper is about these words. More accurately, it is about what these words tell us concerning the Church in our country and our role as religious in that Church.

We understand the task of our Conference as one of calling, enabling, and effecting dynamic action with the aim of bearing authentic religious witness, exerting vocal and visible leadership within our Church and nation, and promoting justice and human rights. This paper represents the shared reflections of many of our members about themes central to our life as a Conference today.

Nothing about this paper is definitive or complete. We do not aim here to state a comprehensive ecclesiology, to articulate a fully balanced theology of the religious life, or to delineate an action-agenda for the religious men in the United States. Some of our reflections will have theological implications, of course, but we cannot develop them here. Other comments will suggest challenges and possible lines of action for the near future; but the action-agenda must flow from the work of our entire membership in regional and national assemblies and even more from the decisions and plans of each congregation. What we hope to do here is to articulate some high-points of a vision of Church and religious life that is emergent among us, to show how and where we hope to be religious today.

CHALLENGES OF U.S. LIFE AND THE U.S. CHURCH

We are deeply affected by the world and the Church in which we live. Our perceptions and our commitments aim to respond to that world and Church. We live in a nation caught up for the first time in its history in a profound experience of cultural, economic, and social limitations. Our history has taught us to consider ourselves pioneers, but we no longer feel confident in attacking new frontiers. Many of us are perplexed by the realization of our power as a nation: we know that this power profoundly affects the economic system of the entire world, but we have not found a satisfactory formula for the best use of that power. One of the key challenges to religious life in our country today is to grapple with the leadership we must exert for the creation of a global society that is more just and human. More and more we are attempting to respond to that challenge.

Within our national boundaries, we confront the continuing social evils of racism, sexism, and indifference to human life. Faltering economic realities (inflation, recession, rising unemployment, energy crisis) alarm our still wealthy nation. We need to redress an inbuilt structural bias within our society against the poor. We are called to respond to a marked breakdown in the traditional societal consensus regarding marriage, family, and sexual morality. The complementary roles of men and women within our society seem to be changing with bewildering rapidity.

Religiously, U.S. society is characterized by the growing appeal of fundamentalism and by an anguished clutching to comfortable but unexamined sureties. Many who still think of themselves as believers feel disaffected or alienated from all organized religion, including the Catholic Church. Our Church does not and cannot present the relatively uniform religio-cultural face of Catholicism in most other countries because it is a multi-cultural Church: Irish, German, Italian, Slavic, black, French, Canadian, Native American, Asian and increasingly Hispanic (Mexican, Cuban, Puerto-Rican, South American). Within this diverse Church the dominant role is played by people of middle class origin, representative of the older waves of immigration from Europe and increasingly at home in the Anglo-Saxon mentality and value-system which have formed our national consciousness. Very rapidly, the laity is taking on a role of heightened significance and leadership within the U.S. Church, but their leadership may appear weak in comparison with that exerted by their counterparts in some other areas of the world.

ON PILGRIMAGE

As a Conference of Major Superiors existing within the complex reality of the U.S. Church today, we recognize a significant development during the past few years in the way we perceive the Church and our role in it. Like the great figures of Scripture and the saints in Church history, we know that we are called to respond to new realities. Yet it has not been easy for us to author this statement. Even though we believe that a pilgrim and prophetic stance is emerging, it is still embryonic. Every sentence needs qualification. We are at best "stumbling pilgrims and stuttering prophets."

The III Inter-American Conference of Religious at Montreal (1977), the Convergence Process together with the Leadership Conference of Women Religious (1978), and our National Assemblies on Domestic Issues of Justice (1979) and Priorities for the 80's (1980), marked high points in our emerging consciousness. As a group, we are still not sure of all the implications; the members of our respective communities sometimes spur us on to further growth in this direction, but just as often confront us with doubt and incomprehension.

We know that we live in a time of unusual transition. We are witnessing a major shift away from a role which gave overwhelming priority to the building and maintaining of Church institutions. We experience internal tensions when we try to delineate clear and vigorous programs of action. Our experience of polarization and conflicting priorities, though perhaps diminished, is still very real. We do not have a clear and precise road map that displays the goal of our pilgrimage and the best route to take.

Perhaps our greatest challenge today, within each institute and as a conference, is that of clarifying, unifying, prioritizing. It is not a challenge that can be met by mere organizational processes; unity and vigorous action will be possible in the measure that we come to share a common appreciation for our rich heritage and a common set of dreams and aspirations for the future. Through the many activities of our conference we aim gradually to lead to clear and effective options for the pattern of our religious life and the shape of our ministries. For the time being, we simply know that we must remain "on the road," not as aimless wanderers, but as true pilgrims.

PROPHECY

Our call to be religious in the Church today is clearly a call to a prophetic stance. More and more, with much qualification and fear, and often with obvious inconsistencies between word and deed, we are trying to measure up to the prophetic element in our vocation.

The Church as a whole has a prophetic role. We religious believe we are being called today to be a concrete embodiment of this role. This call impels us to move out of the narcissism—individual and collective—that readily tempts us. To be prophetic in discipleship of Jesus Christ is to witness to a non-sentimental Gospel of faith, hope, and self-sacrificing love. This is a fearful call, but one that we find ourselves contemplating, perhaps accepting, more and more.

There are many ways to be prophetic; but all authentic prophecy grows out of prayer and discernment and is a following in the footsteps of the Old Testament prophets, and above all in those of Jesus, prophet and suffering servant, who fulfilled the promises of the old covenant and ushered in the new.

For us the real hallmark of a prophetic role in today's society is an effective commitment to justice and human rights. The heart of this commitment to social justice is fidelity to the biblical witness itself, which insists on God's judgment as the ultimate norm for all social, political, and ecclesiastical life.

The basic prophetic tasks are to call the world and the Church to the reality of faith and to call believers to the reality of the world in which we live. Sometimes prophets announce the coming of God's kingdom and point out, to a people tempted to cynicism and despair, the signs which foreshadow it. We believe that much in our contemporary United States reality (an eager search for spiritual meaning, a high value placed on freedom, growing aspirations for justice and human rights, longing for genuine human communion) represents a creative gift of God in our time and place and needs to be affirmed as his grace.

Yet, in fidelity to the same Lord, prophets cannot simply applaud the powers that reign or bless the status quo; often their task involves denunciation and healing. Some characteristics of our national economic, social, cultural, and religious life (consumerism, cynicism, the search for security in fundamentalism or in instant spiritualities, the glorification of material progress, a neglect of the global and national poor) cry out for this kind of prophecy. But we are still timid and not yet sure we know how to read the signs of the times. We have little experience or expertise in social and cultural analysis. Feeling overwhelmed by the systemic complexities of social evil, we find it easier to be silent than to speak. Moreover, we often hesitate because we are uncomfortably aware that even our own institutions and those of our Church can be repressive and unjust, and that they too must hear the prophetic call to repentance and conversion.

Trying to respond to this prophetic element of our vocation, we find ourselves taking a critical look at our own life-style. We know that we too often fall into the comfortable superficiality of much that surrounds us. Ironically, or perhaps providentially, the challenge to a more prophetic life-style is impinging insistently on us just at the point in history when our Church and our religious communities have emerged from the status of the foreign, immigrant, and marginalized, and have been accepted as social and cultural forces of some import. Therefore, conversion to a more prophetic life-style requires the re-examination and sometimes the sacrifice of much that we have learned to treasure in the relatively brief course of U.S. Catholic history.

We cannot expect to be signs of justice and love unless we model them in our lives, individually and corporately. The life of prayer, reflection, and contemplation at the core of our religious commitment can be prophetic in itself, particularly in a society which seeks spiritual meaning but is often content with cheap sensationalism and effortless reassurance. Our vows of chastity, poverty, and obedience offer us a unique freedom and opportunity to take on the risk of prophecy, for they stress the importance of being over doing and having, and they challenge distorted values of property, pleasure and power. More and more we are seeking ways of authentic religious life that will communicate prophetic words of encouragement and challenge. But we know that we still have far to go.

The emphasis on the prophetic role is also beginning to take shape in ministry. We remain committed to ministries in education and pastoral work, but they are taking on new forms. We are seeking to reorient our institutions to a more prophetic role in society. We are beginning to understand empowerment, and not only direct service, as our role.

Since we are often minorities within Church institutions, working side by side with large numbers of others, we are seeking to evolve a prophetic mode of presence with and to our lay co-workers. The concern for the development of lay leadership is emerging as one of our highest priorities. We must increasingly minister to the ministers, rather than trying to do it all ourselves.

At the same time, we are also searching for new ministerial directions in such challenging forms as ministry to migrants, community housing projects for the poor, ecumenical ministries, work in government agencies, and service of marginalized groups: the aged, the retired, undocumented workers, the divorced, the unemployed, refugees and the handicapped.

Ministry is still an area of much tension because of the variance of our visions and options, the insistence of the many calls upon us, and the shrinking numbers of our members. But we are seeking and gradually finding ways to provide community support for new and sometimes controversial forms of ministry and for the reorientation of the old ones.

We must confront many challenges and questions in the next decade if we wish to fulfill the prophetic role. People in general probably do not think of us as genuine prophets. What must we do, what price must we pay, if we wish to embrace a prophetic stance? How can we be prophetic without becoming triumphalistic? How can we be prophetic without losing a ministry to the middle class which is the social origin of nearly all of us? How can we learn to read the signs of the times and discern more surely the thrust of prophecy? What steps must we take to arrive at solid social and cultural analysis? How can we relate our traditional institutions to the prophetic role? How can we motivate ourselves, with God's grace, to accept a materially poor standard of living? We have more questions than answers, but we believe that we are on the way to a new, more prophetic presence within the U.S. Church.

COMMUNION

To be Church is to stand in communion with those who share in the commitment to follow Jesus. Our heritage as communities of people who strive to be religious orients us to live out ecclesial communion in an intense way.

Vatican II has given us an intensified awareness of the local Christian community—the unique way in which faith finds expression in each neighborhood, ethnic group, diocese, region, and nation. We know that our communion within the Church universal is an illusion and an alienation if it is not rooted in authentic local communities which are true centers of shared faith and life. It is here, in the experience of grace and sinfulness within a community on a human scale, that we know Church communion concretely, are called to continual renewal of life, and have the potential to become credible signs of the love commanded and promised by the Lord—prophetic signs particularly needed in a society where millions feel unloved, uprooted, isolated, and unwanted. It is here, on the local level, that it becomes unmistakably evident that no pursuit of communion succeeds unless the members espouse a common mission and that this common mission can be evolved only from a stance of openness to our culture, insertion in it without absorption, recognition of its goodness as well as its pervasive sinfulness. It is in the local communion that we learn to celebrate and consecrate a true communion and life and aspiration, a sacrifice of service, joining it to that of Christ through worship and sacramental life. Thus it becomes clear that the life of each religious community as such has within it a prophetic opportunity.

As we attain greater authenticity and depth of community in the Christian community closest to us, we are prompted to reach beyond to the diocesan, regional, national, and universal Church. An appreciation for these various levels of communion can become a source, not of contradiction and distraction, but rather of energy and life. If our religious communities, our local parishes, our dioceses do not reach out to these broader levels, they will become rigid and stagnant. We are enriched by interdependence.

In the pursuit of a more authentic communion, we find ourselves moving away from the congregational independence which once characterized us and bonding increasingly with others, lay and religious. Our formation programs and our ministries are more often intercongregational. We are learning to work more closely with women religious, diocesan clergy, and lay ministers. We are just beginning to realize that this collaboration is an enrichment not only for our ministries but also for the life of prayer and community. We are taking slow but steady steps toward closer bonding with the hierarchy, common pastoral planning, and cooperation in realizing diocesan and regional goals. At the international level, the CMSM is seeking to promote interrelatedness and interdependence with religious elsewhere, very especially with the Leadership Conference of Women Religious, the Canadian Religious Conference, and the Conference of Latin American Religious. We are often impelled to bond in ecumenical and humanitarian efforts with many who are not Catholic or even Christian. The idea of "reverse mission"—the impact we can have on one another, globally as well as locally—is beginning to have an effect. We are coming to realize that we not only reach out to evangelize others, but that those to whom we are sent (people of other nations and cultures, minorities within our own nation, in fact all people to and with whom we minister) exert a profound evangelizing impact on us.

In our multi-cultural Church, the varied social and ethnic forms of ecclesial life are challenged to remain open to one another for the sake of mutual enrichment. The implications of this reality are affecting us today in a new way. The majority of U.S. men religious are of Irish, German, Slavic, French-Canadian and Italian descent. We have probably not sufficiently attended in recent years to the varied wealth of even these dominant traditions. And for the most part we have neglected other ethnicities. This neglect becomes painfully evident to us when we realize that at least a third of our Catholics are Hispanic (a group extremely varied in itself). Moreover, we have many Catholics among Native Americans and Asian Americans. Black Catholics form an important group; although they are few in proportion to the number of black Americans, we have come to a humbling awareness of the many sins of racism in our past, and we recognize a call to minister much more affirmatively and effectively within the black community. In each culture we are coming to understand that there are unique social, cultural, and religious problems, that approaches to prayer, morality, and Church-belonging are different, that value patterns vary, and that consequently an adequate ministry and Christian life-style must be adapted to each cultural group. The affirmation of such variety and uniqueness and the development of a more authentic religious presence within each culture are important challenges we face.

Another concern of the years ahead will be to continue and extend the steps toward bonding and interdependence we have already taken. We feel challenged to articulate our unique gift and contribution to the universal Church through the development of a genuinely North American U.S. theology, religious praxis, and pastoral style. In order to achieve this end, we need to integrate dichotomies inherent in our tradition between the academic and the pastoral, between theology and experience, between deed and thought. One more key challenge is that of learning how to maintain and enrich our charisms as religious institutes, while at the same time becoming more integrally involved in the over-arching life and work of the local Church, for we wish to experience communion in the manner proper to each of our communities.

The challenges of communion, evidently, remain great. But we have seen much progress over the past few years.

SOLIDARITY

A growing emphasis on solidarity with the poor and the marginalized flows from the efforts we have begun to make at prophecy and communion. We suspect that solidarity will be a key characteristic of the new mode of presence characteristic of religious if we truly take a stance marked by prophecy and communion.

We are still at an early stage, trying to understand the real implications of solidarity. We would like to make a commitment to solidarity with the poor and marginalized that reflects Jesus' own love for them; but we do not feel that it would be faithful discipleship to reject any others. We wonder if there is not some kind of solidarity with the middle class—our heritage—which is incumbent upon us. We know that we should call our nation and our Church to a more effective oneness with those who stand on the margins, but our identity becomes blurred as we try to bridge the gap between the marginal and the majority of middle-class people who fill our parishes, schools, and other institutions. These people are neither controlling nor marginalized. They are manipulated like the poor by the global system of economy and power, but they participate in some of its benefits. At least we are coming to realize that presence through institutionalized patterns of service, valuable as it is, cannot exhaust our call. We feel summoned to share the life of our people—particularly the poor and the marginalized—more directly. We know that we should not stand apart from the victims of injustice, even in a benevolent way, but must move closer to them. We cannot pretend, romantically, to be the same as these victims, but we would like to reach out to them, experience their world, stand with them. Ministry is not a one-way street. We have much to learn from them.

Consequently we are challenged to find life-styles and forms of ministry that place more of us in solidarity with the marginalized. Since we inevitably remain participative in U.S. middle-class life, we need more work in social and cultural analysis to understand the situation of those with whom we wish to stand. In our complex society, it is not at all easy for us to judge such matters in a global perspective and focus on the true causes of social sin. Above all, we need to clarify our options. But somehow we must learn a new mode of presence if we wish not to be absorbed and domesticated by a society which, though deeply shocked by symptoms of decline and by rapid cultural change, remains fundamentally comfortable and dominant.

GOSPEL FREEDOM

To be Church today means to live in the freedom Jesus came to give.

While he was loyal to the Jewish tradition to the very end, Jesus never allowed law or custom to limit his ability to serve. His oneness with the Father and his unquestioned acceptance of the Father's will conferred on him a radical freedom regarding family, friends, tradition, custom, law, temple, prejudice, and power. He respected and cared for all, without allowing anyone to deflect him from his mission.

Freedom is a problem for our society today. In a time of high mobility and rapid change, people are hungering for roots and stability. They do not want to be enslaved by a past which they only dimly know; yet they seek the sense of existential belonging, security, and meaning which only a tradition can give.

Part of the witness of religious life is to live out the relationship between tradition and Gospel freedom in a creative way. For us, tradition is meant to be the foundation for creative breakthroughs. At some critical moments in history, religious have used their unique freedom to break out of old molds and form new ways of response to the Gospel. Our tradition is itself one of radical innovation.

We are called today to celebrate, interiorize, and reinterpret tradition for our own times. We are called to do this on the level of our originating charisms, rereading them in the light of the signs of the times. We are called to go through the same process with the whole of the Christian tradition to which we are committed. If we can respond authentically to that call we can remain both loyal and radical, always the same yet always new.

In this process we acknowledge the need for authority and obedience. We are learning to see the role of authority as that of maintaining and strengthening communion among people on pilgrimage toward a common goal. We are trying to exercise the authority we have within our institutes in a way that recognizes the gifts and talents of each member and calls him to mission in fidelity to the Lord. We know that the experience of being recognized and needed for mission is itself a creative experience, and we seek to develop models of authority which foster this experience.

All of us are also subject to obedience, understood as a faithful listening for the voice of God as he speaks within us and through others. Through obedience we break out of the imprisonment of selfishness and come to share in the wealth of others. Such obedience—the giving of a self that is fully possessed—is a high form of liberation. We are still confronted with many problems concerning authority and obedience within our institutes, but we feel some progress in the move toward a common, freeing fidelity to the Lord.

In this search for an obedience that is truly of the Gospel, we experience an ongoing tension concerning the exercise of ecclesiastical authority. We look for signs within the life of the Church that favor evangelical freedom. We are saddened when we experience any diminution of human rights in the Church. We are concerned at manifestations of authoritarianism. Our advocacy for certain reforms (a fuller role for women in ministry, full development of lay ministries, respect for freedom of inquiry among theologians, pastoral sensitivity to priests who have resigned their ministry, the elimination of discrimination against lay religious within their institutes, the declericalization of ministry in general) flows from our sense of mission and the vision of prophecy, communion, solidarity and Gospel freedom which is growing among us.

A challenge in the realm of Gospel freedom is that of forming our consciences and those of the people who look to us for leadership. It is not easy today to know how to harmonize freedom with the fullest expression of the Lordship of Jesus in our lives. Having broken away from some old moorings that now seem authoritarian, we find the process of Christian decision-making often perplexing. How can we form conscience responsibly and faithfully? How can we best exercise leadership within our own institutes toward freedom and fidelity, tradition and innovation? How can we harmonize respect for ecclesial communion with individual conscience in cases of conflict? These questions have been on our agenda for some time. They will continue to challenge us in the years ahead.

CONTEMPLATION

Jesus lived at one with the Father and the Spirit, and the consciousness of this unity informed the whole of his ministry. Since we know that our religious life is before all else a call to live as a disciple of Jesus and that commitment to the Lord is the irreducible basis of our lives, we have focused as a Conference on the spirit and forms of contemplative prayer. Our contemplative members have taught us much. We have come to understand that contemplation involves a pervasive consciousness of God and a continual discernment regarding the influences that shape our lives.

If we live in God, we know that we will be impelled to reach out to all the cosmos and all humanity in him. God is a sphere whose center is everywhere and whose circumference is nowhere.

The contemplative stance takes on special accents in a religious life that highlights prophetic, pilgrim, and communitarian aspects. We are seeking an incarnational contemplation that discovers the presence of God within the many facets of human experience. We are reaching for a oneness that finds the action of God in those to and with whom we minister, in our experience of human growth and development, in all dimensions of the human community, as well as in solitude and formal prayer. We are beginning to understand that the spiritual life involves participation in the salvation history of a whole people, as well as a uniquely personal relationship with the Lord.

God's saving action and the work of his Spirit become especially evident to us when we encounter the poor and the marginalized. What is marginal to society is central to God. Our movement toward solidarity with them is partly a reaching out to a deeper awareness of him.

Discernment is a key theme of the spirituality that is emerging because of our need to winnow what is authentic from what is inauthentic in all that claims to be of God's Spirit. We are seeking to read the signs of his action and to attain the conversion of heart, inner freedom, and sense of fidelity which are necessary for every genuine prophetic voice.

A concern for the experience of God has awakened among many of our members a new sensitivity to symbolic modes of expression, both within liturgical worship and beyond it. Prophetic words and gestures of solidarity cannot be adequately captured in rational discourse. Here again, the marginalized—especially our large Hispanic and black populations—challenge us by their expressiveness in creative modes which we wish to experience and affirm.

Common worship and personal contemplation are inseparable from our vocation as religious. The people of God look to us for guidance and example in the life of prayer. We are challenged today to maintain and renew the search for a genuine being with the Lord at rest and in action, in solitude and in ministry.

CONCLUSION

In this paper we have tried to be honest. We have not hidden the sinful dimensions of our lived reality. Yet above all we are conscious of the presence of grace and the work of God's Spirit within our Church and our religious communities.

This graced awareness became particularly evident in our most recent National Assembly (August 1980) where we shared a growing consensus about our priorities and a strong commitment to pursue them. We called our Conference leadership and one another to:

- deepen our awareness of the global needs of Church and world to develop responses in accord with our unique role as religious of the United States;
- continue and strengthen our commitment to justice and human rights, particularly in regard to ethnic and racial minorities and to the role of the laity and all women in Church ministry;
- emphasize bonding, collaboration, and solidarity at all levels;
- develop a religious life-style that stands closer to the poor and marginalized;
- emphasize bonding, collaboration, and solidarity at all levels;
- exert a spiritual leadership that goes beyond "management" and seeks to respond to the Spirit of God.

We come to Santiago to call and be called. We eagerly await the reflection of our brother and sister religious of the Americas, for we recognize our close interdependence. In the conviction that God's Spirit is calling us into a new era of grace, we look to the future with profound hope.

IN SOLIDARITY AND SERVICE: REFLECTIONS ON THE PROBLEM OF CLERICALISM IN THE CHURCH

Francine Cardman
Paul Philibert, O.P.
James Provost
William Loewe
David O'Brien
David Bowman, S.J.
Barbara K. Bowie
Veronica Grover, S.H.C.J.

The desire to address the question of clericalism grew out of the experience of the members of the Conference of Major Superiors of Men over a number of years. Initially the problem of clericalism presented itself in terms of attitudes and assumptions about brothers and priests and the relationships between them. Out of a heightened consciousness of the negative effects of clericalism within religious communities emerged a growing sense of its equally adverse impact on relationships with women religious and with lay people.

At its 1980 Assembly in San Antonio, the members of the CMSM indicated their desire to take a serious look at the challenge of clericalism by including it as one of the Conference's priority concerns. The Executive Board then decided to study the question in more depth and to commission a Task Force to produce a working paper.

The Task Force included the following members: Francine Cardman of Weston School of Theology; Paul Philibert, O.P., James Provost, and William Loewe, of the Catholic University of America; David O'Brien of Holy Cross College; David Bowman, S.J., engaged in ecumenical ministry in Chicago; Barbara K. Bowie of the College of Notre Dame; and Veronica Grover, S.H.C.J., Director of the Peace and Justice Office for the Diocese of Raleigh, North Carolina. The Task Force worked from October 1981 until March 1983 in order to produce "In Solidarity and Service."

The focus of the paper is behavioral, not doctrinal. It does not aim to present a new theology of orders but to promote new modes of relationship between clergy and laity in the Church.

This paper is not an official statement of the Conference of Major Superiors of Men. It is a working paper designed as a first step to initiate a process of dialogue, discernment, and decision. Since its publication, the paper has been used to invite other members of the Church to engage in critical reflection on the issue of clericalism.

Many of these readers, including some members of the Conference itself, have found significant points of disagreement with the stance taken in the paper. Nevertheless, "In Solidarity and Service" has proved to be a stimulating and valuable contribution to the ongoing development of American religious life.

INTRODUCTION

The Church follows its risen Lord in his mission of reconciling love for the world. By preaching and by healing it invites men and women everywhere to form a community of love, solidarity and service, reconciliation and wholeness, where the many gifts of the one Spirit are made manifest in the shared ministry of all the baptized.

Since the Second Vatican Council, a new vision of Church as just such a community has begun to take shape among us. The forms and expressions of discipleship embodied by it remain to be seen, the fruits of communal discernment. But it is already clear that the emerging vision of a Church of coresponsibility and collegiality, of mutuality and equality in the Spirit, challenges us to develop new models of ministry that are collaborative, enabling and creatively accountable to the whole community. In this challenge and vision there is great potential for renewing the Church's life and mission. To realize this potential, however, many obstacles will have to be confronted that inhibit the growth of the Church as a community of discipleship. A serious one, which needs to be faced honestly today, is that of clericalism.

What Is Clericalism?

The task force struggled to arrive at a useful working definition of clericalism. It could perhaps be defined most directly as the conscious or unconscious concern to promote the particular interests of the clergy and to protect the privileges and power that have traditionally been conceded to those in the clerical state. There are attitudinal, behavioral and institutional dimensions to the phenomenon of clericalism. Clericalism arises from both personal and social dynamics, is expressed in various cultural forms, and often is reinforced by institutional structures. Among its chief manifestations are an authoritarian style of ministerial leadership, a rigidly hierarchical world view, and a virtual identification of the holiness and grace of the Church with the clerical state and, thereby, with the cleric himself. As such, clericalism is particularly evident in the ordained clergy, though it does not pertain exclusively to it. Persons other than clerics can exhibit the traits of clericalism. Lay people and religious men and women are all liable to the pitfalls of clericalism in certain situations. Generally speaking, exclusive, elitist or dominating behavior can be engaged in by any person or group within the Church. Such behavior is properly termed clericalism when it rests on a claim to special religious expertise or ecclesial authority, based on role or status in the Church.

Although this wider application of the meaning of clericalism should be kept in mind, it is nevertheless important to emphasize that its basic meaning pertains to ordained ministers, who can appeal to the structures and expectations of office in the Church to justify inappropriate attitudes and behavior that are ultimately counter-productive for the Church's life and mission.

At the same time it must be stressed that clericalism is to be distinguished from ordained ministry and priesthood as such. It is neither identical with nor a necessary consequence of priesthood, but a diminishment and distortion of it. Nor is clericalism an exclusively Roman Catholic phenomenon; it can be observed in nearly all the churches, at all levels of ministerial leadership. Whenever and however it manifests itself, clericalism impoverishes Christian witness to the Gospel.

In the succeeding sections of this paper we propose, first, to sketch the historical meaning and development of clericalism. We will then describe two fundamental social dynamics of clericalism and discuss several of its sociological and psychological aspects. We will follow that by taking a look at the way in which Canon Law both reflects and reinforces the clericalist attitude. We conclude with some reflections on next steps, which are really an invitation rather than a conclusion, since the next steps belong more to the readers than to the writers of this paper. Our hope in taking these first steps is to encourage the kind of reflection, dialogue and action that will help create the forms of ministry and community in the Church most suited to its mission of love, service and solidarity in today's world.

CULTURAL AND HISTORICAL SOURCES

The Church is the historical embodiment of a divine mystery. It is given flesh in every age and place by taking to itself particular cultural forms and expressions. It is, in this respect, a thoroughly human society. But it is a society that has been called into being by God's loving plan for the world. Because of this divine call, the Church is constantly challenged to free itself from the limitations of historical and cultural forms in order to reflect God's redemptive purposes more fully in its life and mission. The dual reality of the Church as both human society and divine mystery presents it with an ongoing historical task: to live in and maintain the tension between sincerely embracing the fruits and forms of culture and respectfully preserving a critical and evangelical distance from them. The delicacy and difficulty of this task can be appreciated by even a cursory reading of Church history. When examining specific developments and their effects on the Church's life and mission, therefore, it is important to remember that they can only be understood and evaluated in relation to both aspects of the Church's twofold reality. The goal of historical perspective is neither to forget nor to freeze the past, but rather to free the future.

Tensions in the Tradition

In the course of its history the Church has had to struggle with the dilemma of institutionalization: how to reconcile the legitimate requirements of institutional structure, continuity and stability, with the baptismal call of all Christians to holiness, service and solidarity. Historical studies in ministry and ecclesiology have shown that, as the Church responded to this dilemma at various points in its history, its practice and understanding of ministry underwent significant development. Two areas of tension in this development are of particular importance for our consideration of the sources of clericalism: first, the tension between community and institution; second, the tension between ministry and sacred orders. Some aspects of these tensions were already evident in the New Testament period. Others did not reach their fullest expression until the fourth, eleventh or even thirteenth centuries. Particular historical circumstances contributed to these tensions as well as to the Church's efforts to resolve them. In nearly every instance, positive institutional gains were accompanied by an increasing clericalization of the Church. In the sixteenth century the Council of Trent, anxious about the stability of the Church as an institution, reinforced the clerical culture well beyond the initial conditions which had given rise to it. In doing so it crystallized the attitudes and structures of an earlier age; it made ongoing internal development and dialogue with world culture extremely difficult for the future. It should be noted that one of the significant dynamics of the current renewal of the Church is the restored interaction of Church and culture which has released needed energies for the process of structural change and adaptation. In order to address effectively the problem of clericalism in the context of this contemporary renewal, it is necessary to have some sense of the historical and theological tensions in the tradition which have contributed to the development of clericalism.

Community and Institution

The early Christian community described in the New Testament was marked by an egalitarianism new to the world around it. This fundamental sense of the equality of all believers was expressed most notably in the liturgy and theology of baptism. An experience of the corporateness of salvation in and through the community, and an experience of ministry arising from within it for the sake of service and good order, were central features of early Christian life. As the community grew in numbers and in historical experience, there gradually evolved a complex social structure organized along hierarchical and patriarchal lines. In the institution thus formed, authority and structural continuity tended to weigh more heavily than charism and flexibility. In response to external crises and the strains of internal diversity, the Church sought principles and structures of unity, even uniformity. In the process it began to assimilate many of the characteristics of the social world in which it existed. In so doing, the Church was able to assume new responsibilities within secular culture, but it also lost some of its ability to criticize that culture and its presuppositions. The egalitarian edge of Christianity was dulled as the Church came to accept and reflect the social stratifications of its world.

By the Middle Ages, those in the hierarchy had assumed positions of power and advantage in relation to those below them. The emergence of a feudal social order further helped to fix persons in their sociological place. A static and hierarchical world view dominated both Church and culture, giving rise to attitudes and behaviors which persisted into modern history, some of which would today be called clericalism.

Ministry and Sacred Orders

In the earliest period of its history, the Church's ministries arose in and from the community that had gathered in response to the risen Lord. These ministries were progressively ordered or institutionalized to meet the community's need for continuity of teaching and office. But as the size and complexity of the Church increased over the centuries, Church office gradually became isolated from the people, differentiated not only functionally but also in terms of status and privilege. Thus the "clergy" were increasingly defined over against the "laity." This was especially noticeable in the cultic sphere, where the minister or priest, by virtue of his association with sacred things, came to be assimilated to or identified with this sacral status. The selection and ordination of ministers changed accordingly in form and meaning. The community's action in choosing and confirming a member to serve had previously carried a sacramental significance: in the human and ecclesial activity God's call and grace were felt to be at work. But with the growing sacralization of the ministry there was a strong tendency to consider ordination as endowing the priest with qualities and powers that were vaguely numinous.

One of the consequences of this historical trend was the increasing isolation of ordained ministers from other members of the Church. Ecclesial and liturgical functions, formerly shared by a variety of persons, came to be restricted to those in orders. The diversity of gifts and ministries gradually became "the ministry," exercised almost exclusively in the liturgical realm and given formal recognition and power through the sacrament of orders. The adoption of many aspects of the Roman civil service model for the organization of Christian ministry furthered the creation of a clerical caste within the Church. As the distance between lay people and ordained ministers increased, the clergy tended to relate to lay people from the perspective of their clerical status, while lay people came to accept and defer to clerical authority.

The effects of the developments sketched here are still with the Church today, though their influence has been modified by the specifically American experience of the Roman Catholic Church in this country.

The American Context

The term "clericalism" first appeared in the context of the Church in nineteenth century Europe. Before the French Revolution, the clerical structure of the European Catholic Church that had emerged from the Reformation era was heavily dependent upon the political powers of monarchy and, in many ways, subordinate to them. In the aftermath of the revolution and Napoleon's rule, the ultramontane movement attempted to secure the independence of the Church by increasing papal authority, while also reforming the education, lifestyle and discipline of the clergy. Because the Church was alienated from political institutions of the day, the fear arose that its efforts at internal reform and external independence were directed toward the restoration of monarchy, the reestablishment of ecclesiastical power, and general social and cultural reaction. The attitude thus ascribed to the Church was labeled "clericalism." "Anti-clericalism," on the other hand, meant opposition to the clergy's aim of defining the limits of the laity's economic, political or cultural freedom. This classical understanding of clericalism has obvious affinities with and equally obvious differences from the meaning of the term as it is used in this paper. The experience of the American Church has given rise to the distinct usage that we are following here.

In the United States, however, the Catholic Church was not alienated from political and cultural institutions in the same way as it was in Europe. Minority status led American Catholics to engage in politics on the local level, creating ethnic neighborhoods and building Catholic community institutions, such as parishes, schools and hospitals. Within ethnic Catholic communities, the clergy exercised an important leadership role. But unlike their European counterparts, they were unable to exert the same kind of leadership in civil life. For this reason, European-style anti-clericalism was notably absent from

American Catholic life, even though a fear of incipient clerical power was a common element of anti-Catholic sentiment in this country.

The conflict over trusteeism in the United States was another source of the particularly American sense of clericalism. In Europe lay patronage had meant control of the clergy by kings, princes, civil rulers or aristocrats. In the United States the practice of lay incorporation of Church property raised the fear that republican values might come to dominate the Church in an analogous way. The spectre of ethno-cultural divisions, radical congregationalism, and the loss of doctrinal coherence and organizational unity led the American bishops to insist on controlling clerical appointments through the control of Church property. As a result, lay people were effectively excluded from ecclesiastical decision-making in this country. Strong centralization in the operation of the Church was the rule of the day. Though priests may have been powerful in their own parishes, they were strictly at the disposal of the bishop and were not afforded any of the guarantees or protections of canon law, a fact that was the source of considerable discontent throughout the nineteenth century. While strong pastors were needed in immigrant congregations, the bishops nevertheless saw themselves as central to the pastoral development and unity of the Cathoic Church in America.

The First Vatican Council brought with it a great emphasis on papal centralization. By the end of the nineteenth century Rome had put an end to the nascent conciliar government of the American Church. An Apostolic Delegate was appointed and, in 1899, "Americanism" was condemned. This resulted in a more clericalized Church and in the development of an American Catholic subculture, unified by the disciplined leadership of bishops and priests. The clergy dominated the religious sphere, holding positions of prominence in a large network of associations (e.g., sodalities, Holy Name Societies), which attempted to monopolize all aspects of the lives of their members. The priest's authority, his exclusive claim to the ministry, his privileged and protected status and the assumption of a personal holiness were seldom the object of question or complaint in the U.S. Church in the first decades of the twentieth century.

World War II and the decades following it brought considerable change to the American Church. By 1960, the majority of Catholics were no longer mostly immigrants, members of the working class, or a self-conscious religious minority. The parish priest was no longer likely to be the most highly educated person in the parish. Since Vatican II, identification with the Church has become increasingly voluntary as the cultural supports and constraints of Catholicism have given way in the manner of most forms of Protestantism earlier in the century. Responses to the dramatically changing situation of American Catholicism have varied. In some instances, attempts to bolster institutional strength and coherence have led some clergy and laity to promote new forms of clericalism. Conversely, a shared sense of the call of all baptized Christians to ministry has begun to challenge the former exclusive claim to ministry on the part of the clergy. Moreover, the call to holiness is being seen as a more universal one, and not virtually identified with a particular status or role in the Church.

SOCIAL DYNAMICS

Group Bias

Group bias is a phenomenon common to complex social organizations in which there is a division of labor, with specialized groups performing particular functions necessary to the existence of the organization. Because any specialized group within a complex social system has particular needs and interests of its own, there is a tendency for it to give more attention to its specialized interests than to the common good of the larger body. Identification of the self-interest of the specialized group with the good of the whole is not uncommon. Frequently the group's identification of its interests with what is best for the whole comes to be accepted by the larger body and given an ideological rationale which serves to legitimate the changed understanding of the group's relationship to the larger organization.

Group bias militates against the common good of an organization or structure by alienating one group from another, engendering suspicion and defensiveness among groups, damaging communications, and creating competition for power, status or goods. Where it has worked successfully to the aggrandizement of one group, it often fosters relationships of dependence and powerlessness on the part of other groups. Group bias is a common phenomenon of human societies. It is easily observed in the world of politics, in the professions, in business and industry and in academic institutions. It can also be found in the Church.

The Church is at one and the same time a mystery of grace and a human society. As a human society it is an historical community which is in a continuing process of self-constitution. It becomes what it is in every age by carrying out a wide range of tasks which assure its continued existence. In the course of its history the Church has become a complex, organized society, in which the division has been one of the sources of the historical forms of papacy, episcopacy, ordained priesthood and a rich variety of communities and ways of life. Although some structure and division of labor are necessary for the maintenance of the Church, the Church has not been spared the negative effects of group bias which has clericalism as one of its dominant expressions. The specialized function of the ordained priesthood, as it has evolved in the structure of the Church, has contributed to the emergence of clericalism, which comes into being when the needs and interests of the ordained clergy seek fulfillment in ways which conflict with, detract from and distort the service of the community. When the rest of the body comes to accept the operation of group bias and even to regard its effects as proper, then clericalism becomes a problem not simply of the clergy but of the whole Church. It is worth noting that similar forms of group bias are operative in other persons and groups who exercise roles of leadership and ministry in the Church. Their claims to special consideration or privilege often rest on assumptions that are ultimately clericalist.

Patriarchal Social Structures

Recent reflection on social structures and the status of women has led to the development of patriarchal culture. Out of this analysis have emerged several insights into the dynamics of patriarchy which suggest that clericalism might be further understood by considering its relationship to this social reality. Patriarchal culture is characterized by several features: the institutionalization of male privilege and power and accompanying social mythology to account for it; the social and cultural inequality of men and women and the assumption that this represents the appropriate (even God-given) pattern for all social relationships; and the formation and legitimation of vertical structures of power that are based on the presumed superiority and inferiority of given classes of people. Western culture, as it has been known through archaeological and historical evidence, is, in this sense, overwhelmingly patriarchal in all its forms. Even in the instances where a kind of maternalism has typically been associated with the experience of a particular ethnic or national group, the female influence in interpersonal and familial relationships did not extend to the larger social and institutional structures. Maternalism of this sort has supported rather than challenged patriarchal culture. Male authoritarianism and elitism continue to mark every level of social relationship.

In its assumptions about social structures, vertical power relationships, and the privileges of class or status, clericalism has clear affinities with patriarchal culture. Most clericalist attitudes, habits and patterns of relationship reflect a patriarchal world-view. The negative effects of the interrelationship of patriarchal and clericalist culture are potentially more debilitating in those churches with an exclusively male clergy. Because religion is a significant factor in shaping social order and is, in turn, itself shaped by an array of social forces, it is important to be very aware of how patriarchal social structures and patriarchal religion mutually reinforce each other. The undoing of the resultant clericalism in the Church would also be an important contribution to the shaping of a more just social order.

PSYCHOLOGICAL AND SOCIOLOGICAL ASPECTS

A variety of psychological and sociological factors, functioning on both the personal and social levels combine to evoke, legitimate and reinforce clericalism. Three call for particular attention here: socialization, expectations, and relationships between women and men.

Socialization

Coming to a mature ministerial identity is one of the necessary and positive goals of the education and formation of priests. The challenge of ministerial and religious formation is to foster at one and the same time a deeper sense of identification with the whole Christian community and a more profound understanding and experience of oneself as minister. At their best, seminaries have encouraged and facilitated this sort of growth. But often enough they have failed to do so. Then the formation process becomes a means of socialization into the clerical caste. Narrow identification with this caste and its interests detracts from a sense of solidarity with other Christians. It favors the cultivation of privilege over service. Such socialization generally inculcates and rewards conformity to the attitudes and behaviors of the group, deference or passivity to authority, and substitution of role for relationship, and promotes difference and distance from lay people. The effects of this, as psychological and sociological studies of American priests in the late 1960's showed, contributed to the psychological underdevelopment of many priests. Loneliness in personal relationships and an ambivalent attitude toward authority were among the marks of this underdevelopment.

Clerical socialization contributes to clericalism by creating a culture of isolationism. The isolation of many priests from much of the rest of the Church began in the seminary and has continued in greater or lesser degree throughout their lives. In the past, seminarians did not experience many of the necessities and insecurities of everyday life that confronted many lay people; food, clothing, housing and health care were all givens. Because relationships with women were strongly discouraged, priests had little opportunity to learn to relate to women as persons and colleagues. Emphasis on the distinctive sacramental powers of the priest encouraged a sacral identity, which further distanced priests from other Christians. The effects of this kind of formation are still evident today, particularly but not exclusively among older priests. In many seminaries formation policies have changed considerably, or are in the process of doing so; but in many others they have not. There is even a certain pressure being felt today, subtle but growing, to return to a model of more strictly constructed priestly formation. It would be a mistake, therefore, to underestimate the potential of ministerial socialization either to challenge or to reinforce clericalism.

A policy of accepting candidates for the celibate priesthood who are in their late teens or twenties runs the risk of intensifying the effects of isolation and so contributing to clericalism. Formation structures and processes need to be very sensitive to the developmental task at this age. Foreclosure of the exploration of identity at this time is a real danger. Identity formation entails learning to live with the tension between self-perception and others' perception of oneself, between subjective and objective perspectives, and between the individual's wants and the community's needs. It further involves arriving at a satisfactory identification of one's sexual orientation, a life role worthy of long term investment, and a set of explanations about life's meaning which engender enthusiasm and commitment. The older model of formation, which is to varying degrees still operative today, tended to provide ready-made solutions to tensions in all these areas. Young adults placed in such highly regimented structures quickly learn to defer to institutional solutions in preference to working out their own resolutions to the inescapable tensions of identity formation. Clericalism, therefore, may sometimes be the consequence of a foreclosed identity which has failed to explore the full potential and scope of individual talent and personal gifts and is thus unable to appreciate the gift of others.

Similarly, priests who have not integrated their own feelings toward authority and waver between dependence and independence are not likely to be able to share authority with others or to develop creative forms of mutual accountability.

The experience and effects of regimentation and isolation in formation can also prevent priests from developing significant peer relationships or deep friendships, either with their colleagues in ministry or with women and men in their churches and communities. Several recent theories have suggested that good peer relationships are a function of the capacity to deal maturely with responsibilities. The lack or inadequate development of this capacity, or its frustration by multiple or conflicting expectations, can lead to paternalistic or threatened styles of relating with lay persons. It can also lead to unhelpful or insignificant relationships of cronyism with fellow priests.

Expectations

In addition to the expectations generated by the clerical socialization process, and internalized to varying degrees by priests, the mutual expectations of clergy and laity do much to elicit and reinforce patterns of clericalist behavior on the part of both groups. Clergy have certain expectations of themselves in their ministerial roles, as well as expectations of how lay people ought to perceive and respond to them. These may include a sense of themselves as authority figures to be deferred to, as exemplars of Christian life and faith, as persons on whom the whole burden of the parish and its ministry must ultimately fall, or as the final decision makers, even in matters beyond their competence or knowledge. These expectations are sometimes accompanied by a definite notion of the standard of living and support to which their office entitles them. For their part, lay people often reinforce such expectations, implicitly or explicitly, and by their behavior they signal acceptance and even approval of a clericalist style. Further, because the mutuality of relationship which would foster "leadership for independence" is so often lacking in clergy-lay relationships, it is easy for clergy to fall into a style of leadership that creates and perpetuates dependence. Lay people share a degree of complicity in playing into such "leadership for dependence." Their acceptance of this style of leadership is a kind of "passive clericalism."

There is frequently an unspoken expectation, an unconscious demand, that priests and religious manifest a degree of holiness, generosity, availability and compassion above that of the laity. Such unreal expectations could easily create unrealistic demands on the clergy and make lay people feel free from the responsibility of embodying such values in their own lives. Many priests today are confronted with conflicting expectations around their role. The challenge to be more modest about their functions within the community often goes hand-in-hand with the call to be more outstanding exemplars of the new dimensions of faith expression sought for by and in the community. Preaching and the sacrament of reconciliation are two areas where such changing expectations can be experienced.

Since Vatican II, liturgical celebration generally has put demands on priests for evidence of deep faith and prayerfulness in the ministry of presiding. Expectations can be unrealistically high in this regard. As yet, insufficient attention has been called to ways in which laity and clergy may relate so as to nurture the spirituality of both. This failure to address a mutual need is one underlying cause of disappointment, frustration, feelings of inadequacy, resentment and withdrawal on the part of the clergy. One reaction of priests to the bind of conflicting or unrealistic expectations is to retreat behind the facade of clericalism, where roles and expectations are at least clear. Because increased clericalism is one of the results of the conflict of expectations discussed here, continued and conscious clarification and communication of mutual expectations on the part of both lay people and clergy is an urgent need.

Relationships between Men and Women

The subordinate ecclesial status of women, itself a reflection of their general social status, gives rise to forms of clericalism, and severely distorts relationships between men and women, both at the institutional and the interpersonal levels. General social structures of domination and subordination relative to men and women have translated easily into the Church's institutional life. Here again the links between patriarchy and clericalism can be seen. Linguistic sexism, for instance, has its counterpart in the language of the liturgy, its effects heightened by an overwhelmingly male presence in liturgical ministry. A style of presiding that draws attention to and even increases the distance between celebrant and community is an experience of clericalism that affects the entire community. But in a Church whose ordained ministry is exclusively male, such experiences underscore the double disadvantage under which women labor in a clericalized institution.

Clerics, like other professional men in our society, are often experienced by women as patronizing. Paternalistic attitudes and behaviors toward women are common social dynamics that have been aggravated by the mystique of an all male priesthood. Paternalistic or clericalist styles, however, can also be mirrored by women as they enter into professional positions in increasing numbers. So long as ministry remains tied to vertical power structures, women who enter the professional ministry will be just as likely as men to act in ways that preclude participatory relationships and shared responsibility. Women who are professional ministers, therefore, whether lay or religious, can be tempted to dominate the non-professional out of a misplaced desire to assert and affirm their status. For this reason, the clarification of roles and expectations is of great importance for both men and women in ministry.

Interpersonal relationships between women and men are also adversely affected by clericalism and the structures that give rise to it. Seminary training and the mores of clerical culture have tended to make it difficult for male clerics to relate maturely to women, to work collaboratively with them, or to interact comfortably in social situations. Improving interpersonal relationships between men and women in the Church is a matter of great necessity. But because it is so easy to separate the personal from the political, it should always be borne in mind that good interpersonal relationships do not always translate into increased equality and mutuality on the structural level. It is entirely possible, for instance, for priests, as indeed for other men, who have formed significant relationships with women, to remain uncommitted to the larger structural issues raised by women in regard to both social and ecclesial change.

Most of the features of male-female relationships that we have considered in relation to clericalism in priests also apply, with appropriate qualifications, to relationships between religious brothers and women. Until recently, the life-style of women in religious communities had tended to isolate them from men while also encouraging their acceptance of subordinate status as a theological as well as a sociological reality. A certain style of celibate religious life that was widespread for both men and women until the post-Vatican II era of renewal did much to foster attitudes and expectations that promote clericalism. To the extent that clericalism has strengthened those social currents that work against equality and mutuality in relationships between men and women, its effects have become magnified in both Church and society.

The present period is a time of transition and uncertainty. Women and men are caught in the ambiguity created by two conflicting sets of claims. One claim is the power of traditional roles to structure expectations and vision. The other claim is the community building potential of a theoretically attractive but as yet sociologically unrealized vision of Church. How Christians respond to these conflicting claims will determine the shape of Church and ministry for years to come.

CANON LAW PERSPECTIVES

Among the factors influencing the course of future developments is the current formulation of a new Code of Canon Law. In its revisions and departures from the present Code, as well as in what it leaves unchanged, the new Code will have important implications for the life and structure of the Church.

Law has a conservative function in reflecting long-standing attitudes and practices. It also educates and forms attitudes by the way it organizes legal structures, rights and obligations, and procedures within society. But law is not a completely accurate reflection of a society's life, nor do its prescriptions express fully the complex way people live. Life and politics, the "art of the possible," are only inadequately related to legal codes and regulations. However, an examination of Canon Law, as it relates to clergy and to clericalism, may indicate some of the long-standing biases and traditional structures which support and, at times, inculcate an attitude of clericalism.

The 1917 Code of Canon Law

The Code of Canon Law promulgated in 1917 has set the framework of Catholic life in this century. The Code mirrors the wider civil and ecclesiastical society of its day. It reflects a classically ordered world view, in which vertical structures of power and status are carefully articulated. The dominant model of Church in the theology of that period, and in the Code, is the institutional model familiar since the Council of Trent and well before. The 1917 Code is built on the view of the Church as a society of unequals. In it there are some, the clergy, who are "divinely established" as distinct from the laity. Clergy are formed into a definite state or class, with its own rights and obligations, a privileged class vis-à-vis the rest of the Church.

Clerical privileges include immunity from personal attack and from civil courts, exemption from military duties and various civil functions, and protection from debtor's prison. These privileges belong to the class: individual members cannot renounce them, although they are lost if one drops from the clerical state and is "degraded" to lay status. Religious enjoy some of these privileges too, and are bound by the various obligations which bind clergy. This, in effect, makes them also a distinct class in the Church, frequently assimilated in law as well as in popular understanding to the clerical caste.

Some of the obligations of clergy are related to the separateness of their state: obligations to excel in holiness and to keep a distance from the world by a life of celibacy, buttressed by regulations about life-style: obligations to wear distinctive garb, restrictions on economic and political involvement, and requirements to live in common, whenever possible. Other clerical obligations are related to the work a cleric is to do in the Church: obedience to authorities, fulfilling functions assigned to him by superiors, keeping up in education, performing the Divine Office, residing in the diocese, if a secular, or in a religious house, if a religious. In view of these functions, a cleric is "entitled" to honest sustenance, giving to the clerical state an economic security as well.

Within this society of unequals, the law restricts organized ministry or ecclesiastical office to those who can have power, whether of orders or of jurisdiction. In practice, this has meant that only clerics, for the most part, may hold significant posts from pastor to vicar-general, from chancellor to officialis, from member of the board of consultors to participant in a diocesan synod. Among religious it meant that, in some communities, power was restricted to those members who were clerics, and, among various communities, those considered clerical orders had more influence in the Church power structure than others.

It is worth pointing out that the formal assignment of power to a certain group or groups does not mean that they are the only ones who can make things happen in the Church. Concerned persons and groups are often able to carry out projects and reforms on their own initiative. But even the most concerted efforts on the part of such persons can be blocked by those "in power" who choose either not to exercise their power or to exercise it in a negative way.

Finally, Canon Law sets various penalties which influence the awareness of clergy as a distinct class. Penalties which apply to any Christian are increased in many instances when a cleric commits a crime. Other penalties are designed specifically for clergy, some related to the structure of the caste, others tied to the ministry which only clergy can perform.

Second Vatican Council

In the very different world of the 1960's, the Second Vatican Council was convened. The intervening forty years of theological, liturgical and ecumenical development had brought the Church to quite a different place than it was in 1917. At the same time, social and cultural assumptions were also undergoing widespread change. In this context Vatican II addressed a number of presuppositions underlying the 1917 Code, modifying them and even changing some of the law's explicit provisions.

The Council reversed the presumption about the Church. It is a society of equals, although, within the community, members have diverse functions and responsibilities arising from them. All Christians have a responsibility for the mission of the Church, are called to the same holiness, and are empowered by Christ and the Spirit to work in the Church and in the world to continue his mission.

Pastors are those who serve, putting order and direction into the life of the Church so that its mission is pursued and the communion of the faithful is strengthened. They are not a caste set apart, but in virtue of their ministry of service they do have special obligations and the right to carry those out on behalf of all the Church. Office, the Council states specifically, is not restricted in its meaning, but applies to any function done for a spiritual end in a stable manner.

The Council depicts religious as a special witness to the holiness of all Christians. They are characterized more by the charism of their founder and the witness of their life-style than by the status or class approach of the 1917 Code.

Revised Code of Canon Law

The revision of the Code is intended to implement the spirit and decrees of the Second Vatican Council. A number of significant changes are proposed to do that. The equality of believers is affirmed. Privileges of a clerical caste are deleted. Ministry is not the exclusive domain of the clergy, although they are given preference for offices related to the ruling function of the Church. Religious are to be distinctive in their witness to holiness and charism, rather than as a separate privileged class.

But law is conservative. The 1917 Code's structuring of obligations is retained in good measure; many are not related to ministry, but to structuring a life-style set apart from the world. Religious are still divided into clerical and lay institutes, even though religious life is neither clerical nor lay of itself.

The number of penalties has been reduced, but special attention to clergy in penal law retains the impression of a distinct class. Judgment in Church courts is still restricted to clerics, or at least to a court with a majority of clerical members.

More significant than the provisions of the revised Code will be the attitude with which it is implemented and interpreted. Here is the crucial test of whether clericalism will continue, or be converted by the spirit of the Council. But the achievement of such a spirit is beyond the law itself, and is truly a question of the "art of the possible" in the Church of tomorrow.

CONCLUSION: NEXT STEPS

In Retrospect

We have reflected on clericalism as a phenomenon that takes its first meaning from a style and worldview that pertains especially to members of the ordained ministry, the clergy. But we have also tried to clarify the role that others play in eliciting, accepting, or approving clericalist attitudes and behavior. We have likewise called attention to the ways in which others than the clergy, men and women religious, lay ministers, or others in position of religious leadership can and often do act in a clericalist fashion. In our observations on history and Canon Law we have indicated something of the long history of clericalism and the habituation of all members of the Church to its institutional structures and theological rationales. From the vantage point of sociology and psychology, we have looked at some of the ways in which clericalism is fostered by the socialization of priests, by conflicting or unrealistic expectations on the part of the laity and clergy, and by certain factors in relationships between men and women. Taken together, our reflections have attempted to sketch the basic dimensions of clericalism as it has been experienced in the Church.

It would seem, then, that in its various manifestations, clericalism is proving increasingly dysfunctional for the new situation of the Roman Catholic Church after Vatican II. In the Council documents the Church defined itself in terms of the mutual interdependence, collegiality, subsidiary, and universal call to holiness of all the baptized that is proper to the pilgrim people of God. Clericalism in all its forms militates against the realization of this vision of the Church articulated at Vatican II. For the sake of the ministry and mission of the Church, therefore, it is urgent that we come to some sense of the choices that we must make in our life together as the people of God around this urgent problem of clericalism.

Choices for the Future

How shall we address the problem of clericalism in ways that will help form a more inclusive community of solidarity and service? A number of choices face us as we seek to move together toward the future. The first and most important of these has to do with the manner of approaching the question itself. There is a danger of "we-they" polarization that leads only to mutual recrimination and refusal of responsibility. Approaching the question in this way would be simply counter-productive. The alternative involves a search for common ground and the recognition of a common problem. This choice requires in the first place the recognition that for the discussion to be fruitful, it must involve all members of the Church. In the course of their own work together, the task force has come to see the need for conversation across groups: brothers, priests, lay men and women, religious women and men must all be involved. Clarity about the complex factors that contribute to the problem of clericalism is another requirement of this choice. Equally important is the mutual willingness to accept responsibility and accountability, and to look for new forms and expressions of our solidarity in Christ for the sake of the Church's mission. These fundamental choices pertain to all who would enter the discussion. Other choices and possibilities belong to specific groups within the Church, and so we make some separate suggestions for each group. As a matter of conceptual convenience we consider priests separately from members of canonical communities, though we realize that among CMSM's membership, priests are members of religious orders.

Priests

Fostering attitudes and structures for collegiality is a most important choice facing priests today. Collegial styles of ministry and relationships, as well as the structures to support these, can be developed at all levels of Church life. These can range from peer support groups and ecumenical ministerial reflection groups to pastoral teams and diocesan councils. They can include liturgy planning, homily preparation with parishioners and the encouragement of varied forms of lay leadership. All offer real alternatives to isolated and authoritarian styles of leadership. There are also choices to be made in the area of ongoing formation. Given the opportunity and the encouragement, new insights and motivation, most priests experience some degree of change in personal attitudes and behaviors. Groups of priests must also see the importance of their participation in the reflection and decisional processes that influence the future of seminary formation as well as the development of ministries. When joined in their efforts by other concerned members of the Christian community, their influence can be far-reaching.

Canonical Communities

Members of religious communities, whether men or women, ordained or not, likewise have choices to make in regard to clericalism. It is more than a question of the type of mutual relationships existing between priests and other members of religious communities. More fundamentally still, it is a matter of how the non-ordained members of religious communities see themselves in relation to lay people and how they act on their self-perception. An exaggerated self-estimation would undermine the familial relationships necessary for the ministry and mission of the Church. On the other hand, low self-esteem, lack of assertiveness, or acceptance of subordinate theological or sociological status in comparison to either lay people or the ordained clergy is similarly detrimental to the life of the Church.

In regard to the internal workings of religious communities, the principles and structures of leadership and decision-making, and relationships between and among communities, as well as relationships between communities of women and men, there is much scope for further reflection and renewal. Life in religious community has the possibility of being a rich sign for the Church of the common call to holiness and ministry, of the grace and freedom of the Gospel. Whether and to what degree this sign value of religious communal life will be fulfilled depends to an important extent on the sorts of choices suggested here.

Lay People

Willingness to assume responsibility for the Church, whether in terms of parish life and mission or in terms of working for change in national and international Church structures and policies, is one of the important choices facing lay people today. The concrete forms of such choices may involve participating in adult religious education or parish renewal programs, actively joining in the ministries and outreach of the parish or in social political ministries, or undertaking other forms of apostolic work. Whatever the nature of this ministerial involvement, it is vitally important for the Church that lay people reflect on and articulate their experience, so that they can rightly play a distinctive role as ministers in the Church, in the larger culture beyond the Church, and in society as a whole. By doing so, they can help overcome the inward-looking, ecclesiastically-centered preoccupation of many clergy and other Church professionals, which is often the source of group bias, conflict and division within the Church. Another prime area for reflection and readjustment as necessary has to do with the clarification of expectations in regard to the ordained clergy. In a somewhat different vein, lay people in positions of Church leadership would do well to examine their styles of leadership and the presumptions that underlie them. The essential question about leadership is the same for lay people as for others in the Church: Is its aim dependence or interdependence, inequality or equality, domination or cooperation?

Women and Men

The carry-over from general societal patterns of male domination and female subordination to situations of clericalistic domination is significant enough to merit considerable attention. Issues of male-female relationships cut across all the groupings in the Church. The choices offered here have to do with the kind of community of love and service we envision for the Church, and the way in which the community of men and women in the Church contributes to that vision.

A Beginning

The research and reflection of the task force aimed at a practical examination of the problem clericalism presents to the whole Church. We see this paper simply as the beginning of a process of continued reflection, dialogue and action. It is another step along the way of discipleship. We hope that it will lead to many other steps on our journey toward a Church more fully reflective of that mutual love, solidarity and service to which Jesus Christ calls us by the power of the Holy Spirit.

THE CHURCH IN THE
UNITED STATES AS PROPHET

John A. Grindel, C.M.

John Grindel, C.M. is the Provincial of the Vincentians of the Western Province. He is also a member of the National Board of the Conference of Major Superiors of Men. Before becoming Provincial, Grindel was a seminary rector and a professor of Scripture.

As a participant in the Fourth Inter-American Conference of Religious in Santiago, Chile in 1980, Grindel was captured by the need for societal analysis as a basis for renewing the ministries of North American religious and by the need for developing a style and approach to theology which truly corresponds to North American experience. These concerns are integrated and articulated in the following essay, which has been presented to audiences of religious in various parts of the United States.

The purpose of this paper is twofold: to speak to the need for an indigenous theology of Church for the Church in the United States and to present some of the elements of this indigenous theology, especially with regard to the mission of the Church in the United States.

The development of liberation theology in Latin America, an attempt at formulating a specific ecclesiological response to the socio-economic and political situation of Latin America, has shown both the need and the place for indigenous theologies of Church throughout the world. The concrete situation and needs of the area or country in which the Church finds itself must always play a significant role in determining the structure, role and response of the Church in that situation. If the Church does not adapt to the situation in which it finds itself it will be an irrelevant voice. However, we live in a world today in which the socio-economic and political situations of different areas of the world and different countries vary significantly. Hence, the mission of the Church in these different areas must also take on very different colorings as the Church attempts to adapt to these different situations.

What is presented here is a very personal statement, an attempt to pull together and express many ideas and feelings that have been taking shape over a period of time. The hope behind this paper is simply to instigate some discussion. The thoughts expressed here remain very tentative ones and in no way should be taken as a final or complete word on the issue at hand.

The ideas in this paper have grown out of many different experiences: twenty years of studying and teaching the Scriptures, especially the prophets; two terms as a Provincial Superior which have called for continuing reflection on the direction of the Church and the Province; a growing conviction over many years that something is terribly wrong with the foreign policy as well as the domestic policy of the United States and that the Church must address these problems; a growing sense of frustration with the absence of any clear national pastoral plan for the Church in the United States. The most immediate cause of this attempt to address this topic was the author's experience in November 1980 at the Fourth Interamerican Conference of Religious in Santiago, Chile. At that meeting it became clear in discussions regarding such issues as service of the poor, solidarity with the poor, ministry to the middle class, and relations with local bishops that the Church in the United States did not have a clear concept of its mission that could provide a context for dealing with these issues. It was evident that there was a need to formulate a concept of the mission of the Church for the Church in the United States. This paper is an attempt to contribute to such a discussion.

The paper falls into two main parts. The first part deals with elements of the socio-economic and political situation in the world and here in the United States, as well as some situations in the Church itself that call for a specific response by the Church in the United States. The second part will present some reflections on the mission of the Church in the United States. Preceding these two major sections of the paper are a few words about the purpose or role of an indigenous theology of Church. The paper will conclude with a few reflections on the Church in the United States as a prophet.

I. PURPOSE OF AN INDIGENOUS THEOLOGY OF CHURCH

From the perspective of a Church manager/administrator, there are two purposes for developing an indigenous theology of Church:

(1) The first purpose is to give direction and coordination to those in the Church who exercise ministry in some way and especially to those who exercise it in an official way.

(2) The second purpose of such a theology is to serve as a basis for making decisions on the use of Church resources: people, talent, money, land and buildings.

Unless the Church in the United States has a clear idea of what is involved in its mission, then it is not going to be able to respond effectively to the situation in the world and in the Church itself that is calling for some response today.

II. THE SITUATION

A. *The Situation in the World*[1]

From the very beginning it is important to be aware of an underlying reality, namely, that the prevailing world system, economical, political and social, is rooted in and has its origins in the colonial domination of Latin America, Africa and Asia by the Western European world from the sixteenth century on. In fact, what allowed the industrial revolution to take place was the original accumulation of wealth in Europe that came from the economic rape of the colonies whose raw materials and natural resources were literally stolen by the colonizers. Today, on the stock market in New York, stocks and bonds from all over the world are bought and sold on an international scale; the capital involved in these transactions was first amassed in Western Europe and England and later it passed over to the United States and Russia. As Enrique Dussel says, "that money is stained by the blood of Indians and wrapped in the hides of blacks and Asians." This is the original sin of the present world order, and all who have inherited this wealth and what it can effect share in some way in this original sin and so have a responsibility to correct the horrendous injustices and inequities within the world that have been created by this rape of the colonies. This responsibility today would fall above all upon the United States since it has inherited the great majority of this wealth and because it must bear some responsibility for the continuing

---

1. The present section is heavily dependent in places upon the analysis of the present world situation in the book *Social Analysis* (Orbis Books/Center of Concern: 1983), Chapters 3 and 4, by Joe Holland and Peter Henriot, S.J. However, the author takes full responsibility for the picture presented here.

oppression of the colonies through its transnational corporations, banks, and foreign policies which are, in turn, spurred on by our own insatiable consumerism.

It is becoming clear that what is called for at the present time is a vast and radical transformation of the economic and political structures of society on a global level, a transformation that will insure the human development of peoples. In other words, capital and modern technology must be put to the use of serving basic human needs and fundamental human rights rather than to the development of profit. Profit is the bottom line in business today, perhaps more today than ever in the past. The reason is that for any business to survive today it must be constantly expanding. However, such constant expansion demands capital and hence profit to provide the capital. As long as profit is the controlling factor in the marketplace and in relationships among nations, the human development of people and the preservation of human rights will be put on the back burner, if not lost sight of. This judgment is verified by simply looking at what the desire for profit has led to today.

For a good profit margin there is needed efficient production and cheap labor. In order to achieve efficient production there has been, first of all, the use of more and more technology, i.e., the use of more machinery, computers, and energy. This has lessened the need for labor, thus creating more and more unemployed. Secondly, in order to achieve more efficient production there is a need for cheaper labor. This has led the corporations to go where they can to find the cheapest labor. In our own country all of this has led to plant closings and capital flight as corporations move to those parts of the country where they can get the cheapest labor. This has often left whole cities and towns significantly crippled as the basic industry that supported the town has moved out. Normally this is done without any significant concern for the rights and needs of the local population nor are significant measures taken by the corporations to help the people left behind. All of this is contributing to the development of a permanent underclass in our country, a class that will never enter the mainstream of productive life in contemporary society.

This desire for profit has also brought about the movement of the corporations into the underdeveloped countries, the old colonies. This movement has grown out of many motives. Important among these motives has been the desire to help these countries grow, but the desire to find cheaper labor has also played a very significant role in this movement. Hence, vast amounts of capital have been poured into the third world countries in order to develop industry there and to provide jobs. Real success was achieved in this area in the 1960's. Growing out of this movement have been the transnational corporations, the conglomerates which have holdings in many countries, are highly diversified and operate from a global perspective. While the original movement of the transnationals into the third world countries was heralded as a great step forward, the reality has been something else. This movement of the transnationals has not led to the vast numbers of peoples in these host countries becoming better off. There are several reasons for this. First of all, the profits from these enterprises have not been shared equitably with the people of these countries. Rather the transnationals are taking great chunks of the profits out of the country or the profits are going into the pockets of currupt local management which is often closely related to the governments of these nations. Secondly, the local governments are often enough repressive dictatorships which are supported through the combined efforts of the transnationals, the banks and first world governments in order to maintain stability for the sake of investors. In this process basic human rights have been and are denied to the people of these third world countries and they have become the slaves of the transnational corporations, the transnational banks and governments. Moreover, the needs of these countries and the human development of the people have often taken a back seat to the needs of the corporations implanted there. The results of this situation are that the profits are not getting to the people but only to a marginal few. The people are being repressed, denied basic human rights and becoming poorer and ending up in a worse condition than they were before industrialization moved in. On top of this, in the process of industrialization, the traditional life style of these peoples has been disrupted; they have been stripped of their uniqueness and have had foreign cultures imposed upon them. All of this has taken place for the sake of profit.

What is frightening about the transnational corporations is that there exists no body to govern and regulate them. In many ways they are a law unto themselves and are not always guided by the most disinterested motives. Moreover, they often dictate policy to governments, including first world governments. In fact, if one looks closely one finds that most of our own government officials, especially the appointed ones, come for the most part from the ranks of the transnational corporations and banks. Finally, it is the transnationals that own and control much of the media. What is called for, then, is a vast and radical transformation of the economic and political structures of society on a global level that will insure the human development of peoples in all countries.

The point of all of this for the Church in the United States is that about one-half of these transnational corporations are based in the United States and are United States corporations. Hence, the United States must accept responsibility for much of the inequity and injustice in the world that flows from the operation of these transnationals. The Church must respond to this situation. What makes some sort of response on the part of the Church imperative is that again and again the government of the United States can be seen intervening in the internal life of other countries to thwart any serious national experiments that are viewed as a threat to the interests of the transnational corporations. Normally this is done under the banner of halting communism.

What makes efforts at transforming our present economic, political structure difficult is that it has been divinized and defended as Western "Christian" civilization so that whoever criticizes it is also seen as criticizing God. The symbol of this civilization is, of course, the United States dollar on which it clearly says "In God we trust." The reality, however, is that the United States is a superpower and, as a superpower, directly and indirectly, an oppressor. All that the United States does, even on a domestic level, affects all other nations. All of those who are citizens share this responsibility which includes sharing in the sinfulness of what is done. The Church in the United States must respond to this situation.

The rise of the transnational corporations and the internationalization of capital has also given rise to what is known as the "national security state." The key to understanding the "national security state" is to understand that global capital and hence the transnational corporations will go to wherever the return is greatest. This has put a tremendous pressure on the countries around the world because they are now expected not only to regulate the economic situation within their own boundaries, but also to streamline their whole national system for efficient transnational competition. In other words, it is no longer corporations competing with one another in the marketplace but countries competing with one another. In order to compete efficiently in the world market, countries need to accomplish several objectives. First of all, they must provide cheap labor for the corporations. This demands wage restraints and the destruction or crippling of unions. Second, the states must provide low taxes for the corporations. This demands a curtailment of social services. Third, there is a need to increase governmental authority to use coercive methods to suppress internal dissent and to achieve its competitive goals. While this latter development can lead to dictatorship it can also take more moderate forms, but even these will involve some curtailment of democracy. Moreover, along with all of these developments of the national security state, one finds increased militarization as countries build up their arms as a means of protecting access to their international resources and defending their foreign investments. One can see all of these trends happening not only in other places in the world but even within the United States. Such trends must be challenged.

The ramifications of all of the above developments here in the United States will be significant. What most people are going to experience is that the trend of upward mobility that has created the middle class in this country is now going to shift to a trend of downward mobility for the majority of the population. More and more people are going to find the basic ingredients of the "American Dream" (a new car, one's own home, college for the children) unattainable. The reasons for this downward shift are clear: the condition of permanent inflation rooted in the arms race; the high cost of present technologies in the basic needs areas such as food, housing and health care; the price fixing of the transnational corporations. As people see these things happening around them they are scared, and it might not be too difficult to manipulate them into war as a means to preserve their way of life.

Finally, there are some disturbing trends taking place within United States society today that appear to be supported by the majority of the middle and upper class in the United States. These trends would include: a desire to preserve at any cost a way of life that was often gained at the expense of the poor; a move to reassert the United States as the number one country in the world by taking stronger belligerent stands and through a horrendous arms buildup; a cutting back on welfare programs and aid to the poor so as to support the arms buildup; removing all the government restraints and controls that affect the development of corporations, and so forth. What all of this seems to reflect, and certainly the basis on which it is presented and argued for, is the fear that our standard of living will be significantly lowered if such steps are not taken. The New Right, which has gained so much political control recently, presents the labor unions and the poor as the causes of the problems that are threatening the security of the middle class. In this way they hope to drive a wedge between the middle class on one side, and labor unions and the poor on the other side. If these trends continue, they will lead to increased class conflict at home and possibly war on the international level as people struggle to preserve their way of life. Finally, it is important to keep in mind that though these present developments on the socio-economic and political level that have been presented here will have significant impact on the way of life of people in the United States, the impact that they will have on the third world countries will be horrible.

This then is the situation to which the Church in the United States must respond. Though one may disagree with elements of the analysis presented here, it is clear that there are forces in the world today that call for a response from the Church in the United States. What is needed is a new vision of reality, a new perception based upon the Gospel. People must be helped to critique the present situation in the light of the Gospel and then begin to build a new vision based on the Gospel. The Church in the United States must be involved in this struggle. As one of the great superpowers the United States is intimately involved and responsible for much that happens in the world, including the injustice that is found there. Because those who make up the Church in the United States are also citizens they share responsibility for what its government and its corporations do. Hence, as Church they must respond to what is happening in the world. However, the Church in the United States needs a theology to guide it in its response.

B. The Situation in the Church

The development of liberation theology as an indigenous theology of Church for Latin America has been an important theological event and has had a significant impact on the life of the Church in many places in Latin America. Out of a concern for many of the same issues dealt with in liberation theology some have been tempted to apply liberation theology to the situation of the Church in the United States. This temptation has been intensified by the growing sense of bondedness between the Church of the United States and the Church of Latin America. This sense of bondedness is found especially among religious communities because of the number of United States religious working in Latin America. However, while much can be learned from liberation theology and many of its insights made use of, it is not valid to apply it to the situation of the Church in the United States. The reason is the fact that the situations here and in Latin America are quite different. Liberation theology has been developed on the basis of a social-political system that is different from the system in the United States. In Latin America there is not a large middle class. The United States, on the other hand, is predominantly middle class. Moreover, one does not find in the United States the extreme situations of poverty and oppression which are found in many places in Latin America. The political structures of the United States and Latin America are also very different. In even the most democratic country in Latin America there is not the experience and capability of exercising democratic control as in the United States. Hence, the political system that liberation theology is opposing is quite different from that in the United States. Even more important is the fact that as a result of its life styles, its consumerism, its transnational corporations and government policy, the United States is very responsible for the structures and the situations of oppression in Latin America with which liberation theology is attempting to deal. In other words, the beginning and the basis for liberation theology is from the perspective of the periphery, of the underdeveloped countries that have been raped in the name of God and civilization to support the center, the first world countries. But the United States is at the center and must face the exploitation of the underdeveloped countries from the perspective of the center and as a Church of the center. Hence, even though the Church in the United States may want to deal with many of the same issues that the Church in Latin America must confront, the two churches come at these issues from totally different perspectives.

The Church in the United States certainly understands that it must take strong positions and be a strong voice with regard to United States policy at home and abroad. This is seen in the strong positions that the hierarchy has taken on such issues as Central America, budget cuts that affect the poor, racism and especially the recent peace pastoral. Still the Church in the United States has not articulated a clear theology of its mission that will help it to coordinate and to concentrate its forces and clarify to whom it is attempting to speak. Moreover, while the United States Catholic Conference in Washington often makes some strong and magnificent statements, too often individual bishops and pastors remain silent. Perhaps some of the problem here is that they do not really know where to go or what to do once the USCC position comes out because of a lack of a clearly articulated mission of the Church in the United States. Perhaps much of the same thing is going on when people from the Church speak out against and take action regarding such issues as nuclear power, the arms race, support of unjust regimes, etc. While many in positions of authority in the Church may empathize with those who speak out, they do not know how to use effectively what is happening because of a lack of a clear idea of the mission of the Church in the United States.

There are also some very practical issues in the life of the Church that demand a clear concept of the mission of the Church in the United States if good decisions are to be made in the years to come. The vocation crisis, for example, is calling for a hard look at the way parishes, schools and hospitals are staffed. Decisions on how to use the personnel that are available will flow from concepts of the mission of the Church. Another practical issue is a growing desire among men and women religious for closer bonding and coordination with the local church in the United States so as to integrate better their own mission into the pastoral plans of parishes and dioceses. However, for this to be successful there is the need for the development of a common vision of the Church in the United States.

In many ways, however, perhaps the ultimate problem for the Church in the United States demanding that it articulate its mission is the recognition that the Church in the United States is no longer the Church of the poor but the Church of an entrenched middle class and that the Church itself has become middle class and adopted the values and perspectives of the United States middle class regarding the poor, the arms race, the developing countries and so forth. In this day and age when the Church in Rome is calling upon all the local churches to be churches of the poor, the Church in the United States needs to take a very close look at itself and to rearticulate its mission as a Church of and for the poor and to challenge the values and perspectives of its own members.

The above formulation of the situation in the world and in the Church should make it clear why the Church in the United States must develop an indigenous theology for itself. However, it will not be easy for the Church to develop such a theology of its mission. Aside from the fact that it is difficult to figure out where and how to start such a theology, one cannot escape the fact that such a theology will have to contain a heavy self-critical note regarding the present United States Church and the role of the United States in the world. No one likes to criticize what one loves. Another significant difficulty is the need to hear the Gospel clearly and allow oneself to be judged by it. This demands the ability to be able to back away from present structures, present roles, present perspectives on life and to try to get a good clear look at the situation of the world, of the United States and the Church in the United States in the light of the Gospel. However, it is very possible that the Church in the United States has become so absorbed into the middle class that it cannot get the objective perspective that it needs in order to reformulate its mission in the light of the Gospel. However, it is imperative for it to try to do so.

III. ELEMENTS OF AN INDIGENOUS THEOLOGY OF CHURCH

This part of the paper is an attempt to present some of the elements of an indigenous theology of Church in the United States in the light of the situation outlined above. In the reflections that follow, the main concern is with the "mission" of the Church in the United States. A full theology of Church would take up such questions as the structure of the Church, governance, and so forth. However, the constitution of the Church must flow from its mission. Hence, before other questions about the Church can be dealt with, it is first necessary to define the mission of the Church.

A. Mission of the Church in General

Any concept of the mission of the Church in the United States must presuppose and flow from the general mission of the Church. It is necessary, then, before dealing with the mission of the Church in the United States, to say a few words about the mission of the Church in general.

The Church is "ekklesia," an assembly of people called together for a particular purpose, namely, to make the reign of God a reality. More specifically the mission, the purpose of the Church is to bring all things into one in Christ, to bring all under the rule of Christ so that at the end of time Christ can present all to his Father who will then rule over all for all eternity. From another perspective it can be said that the mission of the Church is to free all people from all those things that hold them back from becoming so one with Christ that all with, in, and through Christ can stand before God in total self-abandonment in the true worship of total love and praise of God. So the mission of the Church is to free all people from everything that keeps them from totally surrendering themselves to God and to empower them to give the worship of total love and praise to God. The mission of the Church is, then, to bring liberation. This is above all liberation from sin. However, sin with its effects not only exists in the human person but it is also to be found in humanly created structures and systems that oppress and destroy. Hence, the liberation that the Church must effect is not only the salvation and redemption of the human person from personal sin but it must also effect liberation of peoples from all those structures, systems and institutions that oppress and destroy and hold one back from achieving full human dignity. The great contribution of liberation theology has been to recall that throughout history God has freed people not only from personal sin but also from those institutions that restrain and enslave the human person. Hence, the mission of the Church is also to liberate people from all those economic and political institutions that hold them back from achieving their full human dignity and exercising their full human personality so that they can stand before God in, with, and through Christ and give God the worship of total love and praise.

The important question is how is the Church to effect this liberation? The answer to this question seems clear, namely, through the proclamation of the word. This is the one task of the Church and all else is to be seen in the light of it. To use the traditional categories of prophet, king, and priest, what is being said is that the primary function of the Church is to be prophet. In the past there used to be a discussion among the theologians as to whether the ministry of the word belonged primarily to the office of king or to the office of priest. The Second Vatican Council, following the clear lead of the Scriptures, presents the proclamation of the word as the broader and more encompassing factor. Hence, the kingly and priestly roles of the Church must be seen as extensions of the prophetic role of the Church. So the Church, then, carries out its mission of liberation above all through the proclamation of the word.

One of the great dangers that the Church always faces, insofar as it is human and in the world, is the temptation to become identified with a given culture and/or a particular economic/political system. While the Church must always express itself through the language and cultural symbols of the people it is addressing—symbols that can be deeply related to the social, economic and political systems of a people—the Church must never become so tied in to a particular language and culture that this particular language and culture are presented as the norm against which all else is judged. Once this happens the Church's perspective becomes narrow and closed, and, above all, the Church loses its ability to stand back and critique the culture and the economic/political system in which it lives. Moreover, in this situation, the proclamation of the word can very easily end up being a defense of and the spreading of a system that enslaves and oppresses. Hence, though the Church must of necessity be in the world it must not be of the world in the sense of letting itself become identified with a particular culture and/or economic/political system. How is the Church to avoid such identification? Certainly a very important means is the one presented to it from the time of Christ, namely, by being poor, by identifying with the poor. Christians who identify with the poor are free in the face of the system. Having nothing, they have nothing to lose and nothing to defend in the system. Only when the Church identifies itself with the poor and the oppressed can it accomplish its prophetic function of proclaiming the word.

Finally, it should be remembered that because the reign of God, which the Church seeks to make a reality, will become a full reality only at the end of time, then the mission of the Church is ultimately eschatological. In other words, the Church is always preaching, proclaiming and striving for what is to come and will never be in its fullness on this earth.

B. *The Mission of the Church in the United States*

The first issue that needs to be taken up is the question: "What is the ultimate concern of the Church in the United States?" It is proposed here that the answer to this question is that the ultimate concern of the Church in the United States is to effect liberation for the poor on a global level. By the "poor on a global level" is meant especially the poor and oppressed in the underdeveloped countries of Latin America, Africa and Asia. By "liberation" is meant primarily political and economic liberation. There are several reasons for saying that the ultimate concern of the Church in the United States is to effect liberation for the poor on a global level. First of all, the greatest scandal in the world today is the oppression of the poor in the underdeveloped countries by a coalition of the transnational corporations and first world powers. As members, as citizens of a superpower that oppresses through its foreign policy and transnational corporations, the members of the Church in this superpower have a special responsibility to effect the liberation of those being oppressed. Second, from Genesis 12:1-3, it is clear that the reason Abraham and hence Israel were called by God, and so also the reason that the members of the new Israel, the Church, have been called by God, is in order to be a source of God's blessings, salvation to all the other nations. This means that the Church and its members have the mission to bring salvation, liberation on all levels to all nations just as God brought salvation and liberation to Israel. Third, if all who believe in Christ form one body in Christ and if what affects one member of the body affects the whole body, then the sufferings and pains of the oppressed must be the suffering and pain of all who believe in Christ. One cannot ignore a festering sore in one part of the body without it eventually destroying the whole body. Fourth, one thing that is very clear from the history of God's people is that the God of the Old and New Testament is a God who is always with and for the chosen people with power and there bringing them historical liberation from slavery and giving them a new life through a passionate caring/suffering. Like this God all who believe are also called to be freedom givers and to effect deliverance from political and economic oppression where it exists. To turn one's back on the oppressed and deny one's responsibility to help them is to reject one's God.

By insisting that the ultimate goal of the Church in the United States is to effect liberation for the poor on a global level, it is not being suggested that the poor in our midst be forgotten. However, it is important to be aware that too often a concern for the poor in our midst can be an easy way to escape and ignore the real issue of the role of the United States as oppressor in the world. Definitely the Church in the United States must work to liberate its own poor, but it is necessary to see that the oppression of the poor in our midst is the result of the same system that enslaves and oppresses on a global level. Hence, the ultimate liberation of the poor in our midst is closely connected to liberation on a global level.

If the ultimate goal of the Church in the United States is to effect liberation of the poor on a global level, then the next issue is: "How is this liberation of the poor to be effected?" It is suggested here that what is necessary is to effect a radical change of mindframe in this country that will lead to significant changes in its public institutions, both government and business, and in the public policies of these institutions. What is needed is the elimination of structures that oppress and the replacement of them with structures that empower people to help themselves. However, first of all, there needs to be brought about a profound change of mindframe in this country. This goes beyond simply changing public opinion on various issues. Rather what needs to be changed is the very perspective on life that is so often part and parcel of life today. More specifically what must be changed is the modern-industrial-scientific perspective on life. This perspective on life has been of decisive influence in shaping the public institutions of this country. In this perspective on life, knowledge is power, and life consists in acquiring enough knowledge to control and predict the world and thereby to secure one's own life against every danger and threat. Also in this perspective everyone and everything are valued for their usefulness and a high value is placed on competence and achieving, on success and getting ahead. In this perspective, then, people have value for what they do or, in its more decadent form, for what they have. People who succeed and are competent are the important ones. Those who earn little and are not competent, such as the poor and the underprivileged, do not even exist for all practical purposes and can be ignored in the formation of policy. This view, then, puts a premium on what is knowable, manageable and predictable. It does not appreciate grace since everything is earned. It is not open to mystery because everything must be explained. It has no place for transcendence because everything must be managed. This perspective prevails in the public institutions of the United States and dominates the marketplace which plays primary attention to competence and performance for the sake of profit.

What is needed is to bring about in the people and the institutions of this country a perspective on life that says that the individual person has value not for what the person can do or has but because God has entered into a personal relationship with each person, offering love to each person, and thus endowing each one with a definite nobility and dignity and with definite rights no matter what the color or language or origin or sex or economic level of that person. Hence, no one can be ignored in the formation of policy. What is also needed is effecting a perspective on life that affirms that human existence does not consist primarily in the capacity to know and control and manage, but rather that real life consists in risking commitments with love, without knowing where they will lead but with deep trust in God's mysterious empowering grace. What must also be changed is any sort of mindframe that uses religion as a form of escapism from life and injustice, any sort of mindframe that does not see striving for the overcoming of injustice, wherever it exists, as an essential aspect of life, an integral part of the life of faith. Another important aspect of the prevailing mindframe that must be changed is a sense of nationalism that believes that the United States must be number one no matter the cost. As our history has shown, such an exaggerated nationalism leads only to a horrendous arms race and a deification of national security that allows for gross injustice. Finally, and perhaps most importantly, the mindframe called consumerism and the associated concept of private property as an absolute right must be changed. Private property, no matter how hard-earned, is something that the individual only holds in trust and which the individual has the responsibility to share with those who do not have what is needed for preserving their human dignity. It is only when such a change in mindframe is effected that there can then be hope that the necessary changes in the public institutions and public policies of this country will take place and that these institutions will become instruments of liberation rather than of oppression.

If the long-range goal of the Church in the United States is to effect the liberation of the poor on a global level and if the Church is to accomplish this by effecting a profound change of mindframe in this country, then the next step is to reflect on the strategies to achieve these goals. While there may be many means of achieving these goals it is proposed here that the Church's primary strategy for effecting them is through a conversion of the middle class in this country. The middle class must be the primary audience for the Church as it goes out to proclaim the word. There are two main reasons for this. First of all, within the political and economic system of the United States it is the middle class which has the clout, the strength, the numbers to effect change within the system. In other words, they have the vote as well as the buying power, and through the use of their vote and their dollar they can effect change in the system if they want to. Secondly, it will be primarily the middle class which will suffer first and the most from the change in life style and the trend of downward mobility taking place within United States society. As the middle class discover more and more that they are not able to preserve their present standard of living, it will not be difficult to manipulate them to support war in order to preserve their way of life. This danger will become even greater if the New Right is successful in driving a wedge between the poor on the one hand, and the middle class on the other hand, so that the third world people are shown as responsible for the change in the life style of the middle class. What will be needed in this conversion is above all a change in the mindframe of the middle class so that they have a deep concern and care for the poor and accept their own responsibility for either continuing or bringing to an end the oppression of the poor. This will demand that the middle class also be brought to understand their responsibility to share their private property and its fruits with the poor and understand the effects of its consumerism on the rest of the world.

The Church is well suited to go out to the middle class as God's instrument in bringing about conversion because it is a Church of the middle class. Hence, the Church speaks the language of the middle class, dreams their dreams and struggles with the problems of a middle class life style. In other words, the Church and its ministers will know from experience who the middle class are and what must be done to effect conversion by reflecting upon what will, it is hoped, be their own conversion experience.

The means that the Church must use to carry out its strategy—the conversion of the middle class—is, of course, the proclamation of the word. This proclamation of the word must spring first of all from a vision: the Gospel vision of the dignity of the human person; the meaning of life as living out a historical commitment to God and other human beings; the Gospel vision of justice, peace, concern for the poor. This proclamation of the word must contain above all a proclamation of the depths of God's love for all peoples, a love which calls for and demands from each human being a deep commitment to God and to one another in passionate caring/suffering and a trust in God's power to bring life through them when only death seems possible. As background to the proclamation of the word there must be a large-scale education of the middle class regarding what is going on in the world and how the United States is involved. The proclamation of the word must then contain a critique, in the light of the Gospel, of this present situation in the world and of daily events. All of this will demand of the Church a high expertise in social analysis and the ability to reflect theologically upon everyday events as a background for this proclamation of the word.

In this proclamation of the word the Church must use the media in all of its dimensions. The Church must become an expert in the media and the use of it and its langauge. If the middle class are going to be converted, then the word must be proclaimed to them constantly and by those means that will reach the most people at any one time. People's minds, outlooks, and perceptions of reality are deeply affected by the media today in all of its forms. The media is the means through which the power of the middle class is manipulated. It seems clear then that the realm of the media is where the Church must be if it hopes to convert the middle class. However, the Church must see the media not just as a tool to be used in the proclamation of the word but also as something that itself needs to be evangelized, for too often the values that the media carry with it are in tension with Gospel values.

Finally, if the Church in the United States hopes to be able to proclaim the word that must be proclaimed today in a credible fashion and with real objectivity and if the Church hopes to have a real ability to understand that to which the word is calling it, then the Church in the United States must become a Church of the poor and be poor itself. As was pointed out earlier, only to the extent that the Church identifies itself with the poor and the oppressed can it accomplish its prophetic function. It is only when the Church has nothing and hence has nothing to lose or defend in the system that it can step back and take an honest look at the system. The institutional Church, then, must divest itself of its unneeded wealth. As long as the institutional Church maintains and manages wealth it remains an integral part of the system and cannot be independent of the system, free of its pressures and temptations, and hence be a credible voice for the poor.

As a Church of the poor the Church in the United States must also be deeply involved with the plight of the poor in its midst, stand with them in their struggles, and do all it can through the proclamation of the word to empower the poor in their attempts to deal with their situation. The Church in the United States will have credibility before the world only if it first lives out the Gospel message of justice and cares for the poor in its midst. Moreover, only by identifying with the poor in its midst and becoming poor with them will the Church come to understand and see even more clearly the system that oppresses. Even more importantly, by identifying with the poor the Church may also learn from the poor what its real values should be.

The solidarity with the poor that is being called for here is difficult. People would much prefer simply to practice charity toward the poor. However, it is important to remember that Jesus saved us not by practicing charity toward us but by becoming one of us, entering into solidarity with us, suffering with us so as to empower us to be able to take responsibility for ourselves. In the same way we must enter into solidarity with the weak, the poor and the powerless and become vulnerable with them and suffer with them in order to help them gain economic and political freedom so that they can care for and take responsibility for themselves.

IV. THE CHURCH IN THE UNITED STATES AS PROPHET

The conclusion to all that has been said is that the Church in the United States is called to be a prophet, a prophet to the people of its own country. As a prophet the Church must proclaim God's word clearly, unequivocally and without compromise. What is to be proclaimed is a word that will effect liberation for the poor and the oppressed, a word that contains a clear vision of what it is that the Lord is calling for. Moreover, like the Old Testament prophets, the Church is called upon to interpret history. In other words, the Church is called upon to explain in the light of the word the meaning of the past for the present, what it is that the Lord now calls for, and how the present situation in history fits into God's overall plan. Certainly one of the major roles of the prophets in Israel's history was, in a sense, to keep the institutions of their time "on their toes." The role of the prophet was to interpret the policies, the programs and the actions of the various institutions in the light of God's will and to critique them. In a real sense the prophets were the conscience of Israel. In the same way the Church in the United States is called to be the conscience of the United States. The ultimate purpose of this proclamation of the word now, as for the biblical prophets, is to bring people to repentance and conversion or at least to speak the word that forces people to take a stand for or against God's will and so seal their own fate.

The biblical prophets often encountered pain and suffering in carrying out their mission. This suffering was caused not only by rejection and even attempts on their life but especially by the fact that they were children of their own time, part of the people to whom they were called to speak their harsh judgments. Hence, the Church in the United States should not be surprised when it encounters rejection and probably even persecution and when it finds it difficult to speak harsh words of judgment on its fellow citizens. However, this is all part of being a prophet.

The prophets of Israel came to know God's will and their own call to be a prophet through an experience that is probably best compared to a mystical experience. It was an experience of oneness with God in which God's mind and will entered in and took over the mind and will of the prophet. As a result of this experience the prophet not only knew God's will but he became extremely sensitive to the realities of life that surrounded him and was able to see clearly what was in keeping with God's will and what was not. This experience broke the prophet out of his old mindframe and let him see things around him in a completely different light. It was this experience of God that also gave the prophet courage and in fact made him a fearless proclaimer of God's word, because as a result of this experience the prophet had no doubt concerning God's will for the people or himself.

People today cannot hope for the same experience of God that the prophets had. However, this experience of the prophets points out what is important for those who would be prophets today. First and foremost the proclamation of God's word must be rooted in contemplation. Only if people allow God to enter into their life and experience God as someone very real and personal will they not only find the courage that they need but even more importantly begin to be able to break out of their present mindframe as the result of a larger vision. Only through contemplation can one begin effectively to become detached from oneself in the sense of being able to step back and see oneself as one is and be able to judge the perspective out of which one is coming.

Notice that the concern here is not with the necessity of meditation and reflection. While these are certainly important and must be part of every person's life, the point here is that unless people open themselves to the experience of God in contemplation they will probably not break out of themselves simply through meditation and reflection. The reason is that in meditation a person is simply using his or her present mindframe as a context for thinking about God. Hence, a person is not going to break out of his or her present mindframe by staying only with meditation and reflection. What will be necessary along with contemplation will be solitude, taking time with oneself so as to come to know oneself and to understand the forces that have formed one and direct one. Only then will people be able to evaluate themselves and allow themselves to be judged by God's word. Only then can a person be a real prophet.

As was said in the beginning the thoughts that have been presented here are very tentative ones. It is hoped that the vision of the Church presented here makes some sense. However, the author will be very happy if this paper achieves nothing more than getting people to think about the need for and what might go into an indigenous theology of Church for the Church in the United States.

OUR SEARCH FOR GOD

Peter J. Henriot, S.J.
Alan McCoy, O.F.M.
Thomas E. Clarke, S.J.

Over the years, the Annual Assemblies of the Conference of Major Superiors of Men have been significant in developing the reflection of the Conference and in stimulating directions for leadership within religious communities. The Annual Assembly held at Boston College in August 1983 was a particularly important one.

Turning from a series of annual meetings devoted to the mission of men religious in the Church, the 1983 Assembly devoted its attention to the emerging spirituality undergirding new developments in religious life. In many ways, this Assembly provided an integration of themes which appear elsewhere in this book.

The three speakers spoke fraternally to their fellow religious. It has seemed best to preserve the familiar, thought-provoking language of their oral presentations.

Peter J. Henriot, S.J. is the Director of the Center of Concern, an important social-justice institute headquartered in Washington, D.C., which has exerted great influence on religious communities across the United States in recent years.

Alan McCoy, O.F.M. was President of the CMSM from 1976 to 1982 and Minister Provincial of the Santa Barbara Province of the Order of Friars Minor from 1967 to 1976. Presently Father McCoy is serving as a member of the Consultation Committee for the study of religious life in the United States commissioned by Pope John Paul II.

Thomas E. Clarke, S.J. is a theologian and writer whose presence to men and women religious throughout the United States has been particularly appreciated for the past decade.

Peter J. Henriot, S.J.
OUR SEARCH FOR GOD IN THE WORLD

It is always unwise, even a little dangerous, to begin with a very old joke, especially when it is a very bad joke. But there just happens to be a joke—very old *and* very bad—which makes so well a point I want to begin with that I must at least take the risk of making passing allusion to it. It is the story of the very inebriated gentleman who was down on all fours under a bright street light on the corner, searching for something. When asked by a passing police officer what he was searching for, he explained that he had lost his keys down the block a ways. And when the officer asked why he wasn't searching for the keys down the block, then, he explained: "Officer, the light is much better up here on the corner!"

The point of this old, bad joke seems to me to have relevance to the theme, "Our Search for God as U.S. Men Religious." Most of us have probably experienced that it is easy to search for God where the light seems brightest, even though if we are honest with ourselves, we sense that God might better be found down the block a way. Alan, Tom, and I will be casting some light to assist in the search for God. But you, in your periods of prayer, reflection and sharing, may find God in other places. And your own experience of finding God as U.S. religious is really the primary point. This experience is ultimately what you bring in your leadership position to the brothers of your community.

I want to share my reflections on "Our Search for God in the World." "In the world," obviously, does not imply that "fellowship" (which Alan will address) and "solitude" (which Tom will address) are somehow "out of the world." Fellowship and solitude do not exist in a vacuum. But my concentration is more on the public, social, societal, structural existence and experience we have, and where we find our search for God. I've decided to focus primarily on what I consider to be the marks of our search, the characteristics which may make it effective particularly here in the United States at this moment. The search is marked by (1) analysis, (2) action, and (3) affection. Each of these can be seen in the call expressed in a particular passage of the Gospels, a passage I would like to read and then pause for a moment to let you be in touch with how the Spirit moves within you.

1. ANALYSIS

The Pharisees and Saducees came along, and as a test asked him to show them some sign in the sky. He gave them this reply: "In the evening you say, 'Red sky at night, the day will be bright'; but in the morning, 'Sky red and gloomy, the day will be stormy.' If you know how to interpret the look of the sky, can you not read the signs of the times?" (Mt 16:1-3).

The call to "read the signs of the times" is the call to contemplate God's action in history, to discern God's presence in the world around us. It is the call to that contextual contemplation and societal discernment which today goes by the name of "social analysis."

As the co-author of a popular book on social analysis, I might very well be expected—indeed, suspected—to introduce that theme early in my presentation. But let me explain my emphasis by pointing to its theological foundation: our belief in a God who is at once Creator and Re-Creator.

God's action in history is creative, in the act of breathing being and life into all that is. But in the Hebrew Scriptures, God's creative action is not a "once-and-for-all-time" event; it is on-going. It is not removed, disinterested; it is engaged, involved. And so Deuteronomic history reveals that God acts creatively in the secular events which shape the history of Israel; and the prophetic literature reminds the chosen people that God treats with them even through the actions of their enemies.

In the Christian Scriptures, we see the re-creation, which is the act of redemption, occurring in the entry into history of God in the person of Jesus. In Jesus, "the goodness and loving kindness of God appeared" (Tit 3:4). This recreative/redemptive act is not simply the crucifixion, but all the events of the paschal mystery, the life, death, and resurrection of Jesus. When Jesus challenges the Pharisees and Saducees to read the signs of the times, he invites them to pay attention to the signs of re-creation present in the healing of the sick, the giving of sight to the blind, the feeding of the hungry, the raising of the dead, the preaching of the good news to the poor, the challenging of the conditions of injustice. These events of the paschal mystery continue, of course, in the ministry of the Christian community today, indeed, wherever the actions of love, mercy and justice are present in our world.

To read the signs of the times, then, requires attention to what is going on around us, the unfolding of history, for it is in history that God acts. In his *Pacem in Terris* of more than twenty years ago, Pope John XXIII pointed to three of those signs in our contemporary world: the rise of workers to claim their rights, the rise of the new nations to claim their dignity, and the rise of women to claim their equality.

Our search for God in the world demands of us, therefore, a deep understanding of what is going on in the social, economic, political and cultural events and structures of our day. This, of course, is the task of social analysis, the opening up of a situation by probing its history, structures, values and direction, providing a holistic interpretation of what is going on. I certainly do not say that social analysis reveals God. I have experienced, in workshops in this country and overseas, how people come alive with new vision, new power, when they engage in social analysis. And so I do emphasize that it is a propaedeutic, a necessary tool for grasping reality more profoundly and hence for discerning God's presence in history.

I say this for at least two reasons. First, social analysis obliges us to attend to all the elements of a situation, to leave uncovered no stance in the search for meaning, in a genuinely interdisciplinary approach rooted in experience. There are no a priori's unexamined, no corners unexplored, in an authentically critical analysis. Thus, for example, God's action in history may be seen in the sometimes hidden struggle of minorities for their rights, or in the seemingly "secular" dimensions of the worldwide peace movement. We see more clearly what it means in the concrete to say that God's creative and re-creative action continues in history. We can discover hope, and begin to discover the seeds of new life, and thus come to see more clearly the face of God.

Second, social analysis points to those factors in our culture which block God's presence, which account for God's seeming "absence." This is especially important for us in the United States, where in our efforts to assure that the faith be *enculturated*—placed genuinely in the heart of our culture—we must always face the danger that the faith be *acculturated*—become simply a part of the American way of life. Following Christ in a consumer society, as John Kavanaugh has reminded us, constantly requires that we challenge the individualism which obscures God's communal face, the consumerism which hides God's simplicity, the militarism which blocks God's humanism, the racism and sexism which violates God's image, the noise which drowns out God's voice. Social analysis for us in the United States must in particular be cultural analysis, for those elements in our culture which hinder our search for God must be exposed, unmasked, demythologized.

I am suggesting first, then, that we find God by contemplating the world today in a way which strives to understand deeply what is going on, where grace is stirring, where sin is festering, where new life is opening. And we are helped in this through a stance of analysis.

But an analytic stance is insufficient in itself in the search for God in our world today. We must turn to action to give our search vitality and authenticity.

2. ACTION

The next day John was there again with two of his disciples. As he watched Jesus walk by he said, "Look! There is the Lamb of God!" The two disciples heard what he said, and followed Jesus. When Jesus turned around and noticed them following him, he asked them, "What are you looking for?" They said to him, "Rabbi (which means Teacher), where do you stay?" "Come and see," he answered (Jn 1:35–39).

The call "Come and see" contains a powerful lesson, subtle but also obvious. We only see in the coming, we only find in the following. The turn to action is a turn to knowledge and is essential in the search to find God in our world today.

To find God, we need to find Jesus. This is the good news learned by the first disciples who heard the words, "Those who see me see also the Father." Where do we find the face of God in our world today? To answer that we must of necessity search for Jesus.

In his *Spiritual Exercises,* Ignatius of Loyola invites the retreatant to begin her or his contemplations of the mysteries of the life of Jesus with the simple prayer to know Christ better that I might love him more and thus come to follow him more completely.

That triadic progression—know, love, follow—is sacred in the tradition of spirituality. But it is also challenged today, challenged by an epistemology which emphasizes praxis and by a psychology which stresses development through commitment. Perhaps the triad is more accurately stated: follow, love, know. My prayer, then, is that I might follow the Lord more faithfully in order to deepen my love for him and come to know him better.

This reversal—turning Ignatius on his head, if you will—is powerfully suggested by Jon Sobrino in his *Christology at the Crossroads.* Sobrino argues that we know Jesus only in committing ourselves to follow him in the service of God's reign or kingdom. "Come and see— *come and see!*" A praxis approach to knowledge always roots us in action and commitment precedes intimacy. Action and commitment to that work of justice and peace which is central to Jesus' mission of building the reign is itself a necessary step along the road to finding God in our world. This, it seems to me, is what "contemplation in action" is all about these days. At least it has been my experience and that of many others, religious and lay, who I know are struggling for the integration of faith and justice.

Why should this be so? In struggling to answer this, I am reminded of something I heard once in a discussion of world religions. What makes Christianity unique among world faiths is not that we go to God, for all religions offer this path. Rather, in Christianity, God comes to us, in the person of Jesus.

Much the same point is made, I believe, in Paul's Letter to the Philippians: "It is not that I have reached it yet, or have already finished my course; but I am reaching to grasp the prize if possible, since I have been grasped by Christ Jesus" (Phil 3:12). In committing ourselves to action in our search for God, we discover that the one who is really searching is God! God is reaching out for us, coming to us in those moments of identification—our active identification—with Jesus in the work of the reign. In our searching, we are found. This is true "integration" of faith and justice.

This has significant implications, I believe, for religious leadership today in the United States, specifically for you, the members of the CMSM. Today in this country the search for God in our world requires a "contemplation in action" which leaders facilitate through example and encouragement. The "risk" of your taking some action on behalf of justice is essential to community leadership because it models the path to a community's being "found" by God who searches in Jesus. This leadership is genuinely "prophetic."

I am suggesting here, then, as my second point, that we find God in our world by engaging in a following of Jesus through the action of building up a reign of justice and peace, through the commitment which opens us up to being found, being grasped.

But action as a stance is also itself insufficient in the search for God in our world today—insufficient even when joined to analysis. We must also speak of the stance of affection. And it may well turn out that our last word is in fact the first word.

3. AFFECTION

Then the just will ask him: "Lord, when did we see you hungry and feed you or see you thirsty and give you drink? When did we welcome you away from home or clothe you in your nakedness? When did we visit you when you were ill or in prison?" The king will answer them: "I assure you, as often as you did it for one of my least sisters or brothers, you did it for me" (Mt 25:37–40).

The call to serve the *least* is a call to love. It is, in contemporary terms, a call to make an option for the poor. My third point is, then, that the search for God in our world requires the affective stance of solidarity with the poor.

In a very provocative recent essay on the hermeneutic privilege of the poor, Monika Hellwig explores the claim that being poor gives one an advantage in understanding the good news of salvation. Reviewing both the literature of professional theologians and the experience of activists working with the poor, Hellwig concludes that the Gospel proclaimed to the poor is in fact heard by them, received by them, in a fashion which gives them privileged access to the depths of its meaning. Among the reasons for this conclusion are: the poor know that they are in urgent need of redemption; the poor know not only their dependence on God and on powerful people but also their interdependence with one another; the poor rest their security not on things but on people; the poor expect little from competition and much from cooperation; when the poor are exposed to the Gospel, they interpret it very concretely and readily see it as having historical, practical import; when the poor have the Gospel preached to them, it sounds like good news and not like a threat or scolding.

But what does this say to our search for God in the world? When the Puebla documents of the Latin American Church speak of the "preferential, but non-exclusive, option for the poor," they emphasize that the Church simply must follow the example of Jesus in his birth, life, ministry, death and resurrection. Solidarity with the poor is the style of the incarnation. It is not "option" in the sense of a *noun*—such as the many "options" on a new car (air conditioning, white sidewall tires, etc.), but "option" in the sense of a *verb*—a conscious choice to be with, on the side of, from the place of, the economically disadvantaged who are oppressed and powerless. Why? Because this is where Jesus is.

Our search for God in the world—especially here in the United States—must therefore necessarily include the option for the poor. I want very much to stress this here during this first session because in recent months I have experienced a feeling, an uneasiness, that we religious in the United States may be in a mood of retreat from this strong call for solidarity with the poor. This retreat may come for both good and bad reasons. It is good, I believe, that we relativize the call, not see it as so absolute that all other dimensions of ministry pale into insignificance; and it is good that we in this country be newly sensitive to the situation of the middle class in our culture. And yet it is certainly bad, this retreat, if induced by the generally pervasive mood of a country grown weary of publicly caring for its impoverished elderly, its inner city families, its rural migrants, its large number of unemployed, its undocumented. Indeed, grown weary of hearing about the impact on the poor campesinos of Nicaragua and El Salvador of U.S. backed and armed military actions, many are content with merely saying, "The poor you have always with you." Jesus made this remark as an empirical observation, but our current government tends to raise it to the status of a political platform, a basis for policy.

But whether for good or bad reasons, a retreat from the option for the poor is always a block in our search for God. When we sing, "God hears the cry of the poor," we recall the Exodus story of God's appearance to Moses in the burning bush: "I have heard the cry of my people" (Ex 3:7). God promises liberation, the changing of the structures of oppression. That God who was so close to his people, the poor, oppressed and powerless Israelites, is the same God who in Jesus identifies with the hungry, the thirsty, the homeless, the naked, the imprisoned, the least of our brothers and sisters. To pull back from our solidarity with them is in effect to pull back from God—to curtail effectively our search for God in our world.

Yet the option for the poor is only an opening to God when it is affective, loving, and only realized when we are able to stop speaking of "the poor," and begin speaking instead of John and Mary, Juan y Maria. To personalize the poor is to take the affective stance. To personalize the poor requires contact with persons whose names we know, whose lives touch us.

I make a point of this, because I feel it continues to be a profound challenge to U.S. religious, a challenge that has particular relevance to our search for God. As leaders of religious communities, you know this better than I do. Perhaps we—I—need to practice more creatively what Father Pedro Arrupe, S.J. spoke of a few years ago when he was serving as President of the Union of Superiors General in Rome: a "tithing of time" with the poor. Some religious should spend *all* of their time with the poor, but all religious should spend *some* of their time with the poor. Tithing an hour a week, a day a month, a week a year, whatever—locating ourselves, creating our geography, with John and Mary, Juan y Maria. This will lead us—they will lead us—to action on behalf of justice, to changing the structure of oppression. Our God hears the cry of the poor. Do we? Can we?

I know in my personal history when I've missed the cry of the poor, and have thereby been blocked in my search for God. Let me share a personal experience. Several years ago I was studying Spanish in Bolivia. One weekend I accompanied an older Jesuit brother to an orphanage for poor boys. The youngsters clamored all about this *gringo*, enjoying my faltering Spanish. One was particularly insistent to get my attention, but because he appeared retarded and slow of speech, and very poor, I tended to ignore him. I turned to the others who, I reasoned, could help me improve my language. The youngster in question finally latched on to the Jesuit brother, who picked him up and asked him, "¿Como te llamas, niño? What's your name, little boy?" I remember to this day the struggling response of this child: "Me llamo Jesús. My name is Jesus." I've recalled that incident many times since then, when I've turned away from opportunities of solidarity with the poor, from the personal love of those least of my brothers and sisters, and have thereby faltered in my search for God in our world. Perhaps you have had similar experiences.

And so I make my third point by suggesting that we find God in the world today through loving persons with whom he has especially identified himsef, through an affective stance of the option for the poor.

The stances of analysis, of action, of affection: I conclude my reflections by repeating my opening remarks that I offer these as notes or characteristics of our search for God in the world. We find God through reading signs of the times, coming and seeing, serving the least. In your prayerful reflection, you might ask yourself whether you have been assisted in your search of God:

- through an analysis which helps reveal God's action in history?
- through a commitment to be about action on behalf of justice, the work of Jesus?
- through a love of the poor which personalizes the meaning of structural injustice?

My brothers, it's an exciting, grace-filled search, and one in which it's a privilege to share.

Alan McCoy, O.F.M.
FINDING GOD IN FELLOWSHIP

In recent years religious studies have searched for ways to appreciate the uniqueness of the individual, accenting the personal dignity, rights, and responsibility as well as the call to human fulfillment of each one called to the vowed life. Interpersonal relationships were much in focus in this. But even as we searched for this human growth of the individual on his or her way to the fullness of life, it became evident that there was a call to something beyond independent living, beyond that stage where one could try to make it alone, as we say. Fellowship, yes, even genuine community, has emerged clearly as the basic value we are called to pursue in a Christian and especially in a religious life. We are communitarian by nature, conceived and born in and through human community. We are born of parents in and through the Church, the community of believers, the body of Christ. As those called to celibate commitment we are in a more intimate community, sharing a charism, a patrimony with others united with us in life and mission.

Our ability to serve the larger Church and world community depends to a great extent on our ability to enter into a genuine growth pattern within the religious community, local and provincial, in which we are called to live the values of the so-called evangelical counsels through the religious vows.

Particularly as religious the communitarian aspect of our calling is prior to all others. Here is a privileged place to meet God. All experience of him is mediated. In his plan, this mediation is primarily through others, those who call us, challenge us, affirm us, search with us, heal us. Here is where he reveals himself as a God whose call is one of love. And since all of us are under a law of growth, this call entails a growth in relationship with others, even as we aspire to grow deeper in our relationship with him.

Certainly we find God in solitude and also in the larger world, but never if we do not find him in our communities, in those with whom he has placed us for our growth as human beings. All personhood is constituted by relationships. And our effectiveness as ministers, as those who accept a true mission from Christ, will reflect the experience of God in genuine fellowship, within our primary community. What we are to others is more important than what we do for them.[1] And I cannot come to any maturity in my personal life except through a deepening of the relationships to which I am called. Some years ago I experienced a terrible example of the lack of such relationship in the very heart of the family. A young man who had been deeply involved in Catholic Action of the time called and asked if he could come in to speak with me along with a young woman whom he loved very much. He said he would like to marry her, but could not because she could not believe in God. They came and told me her story. As a youngster who attended Catholic schools and religious instructions, she could not accept any truth about God. When God was presented as a loving Father, she could not believe. She received First Holy Communion, but without belief. When I questioned her about her family life, she told me that she was an unwanted child, and this became evident to her very soon in life. There was no love for her on the part of father or mother. Only one of her grandparents showed any love, and she was at such a distance from her home that this meant very little to the girl. I assured her that I could not prove to her that God existed as I could that two and two made four, but asked if she could believe if I could do this. She said no. She said she could not believe no matter what might be proven logically. Not finding God in the heart of her own family, not finding love there, she could not find him anywhere else.

The religious life is a call to a relationship of maturing individuals who are able to enter into interdependence, sharing their strengths and weaknesses in a community of Christian caring, but one fully and immediately open and destined for mission. If we as religious can establish a truly vibrant community within our own religious group, we are prepared to enter into the community of the larger Church and even the world in a life-giving reality. The call to mission, the need to enter into the work of the kingdom of God in this world, the call to face structural and societal sin, armed with the grace of Jesus the Christ, in no way diminish but rather enhance the role of the community in the life of a religious.

---

1. Pope John Paul II, Message to Plenary Assembly of SCRIS, March 1980.

We, as religious men in the United States, are faced with the fact that our cultural roots work against an honest evaluation of the true role of community in our relationship to God. In our Puritan ethic, dominant through almost the first two hundred years of our history, there was no essential role for community in our relationship with God. We Catholics here have bought into this as few other groups. Yet we know that our Catholic heritage speaks out against this. The first thing recorded of God's reflection on humanity, the first "not good," was loneliness. And this reflects the danger of the independent person, falling miserably short of the maturity of interdependence. From the very start we are called to community. It is through community that we are saved and can be a vital part of the mission of salvation in its broadest sense. Just as the absence of genuine solitude can lead to loneliness, so also the lack of genuine community, a growing relationship within a primary community as well as within the larger community, can bring a sad and deadly loneliness into life. And this latter in turn keeps one from a truly fruitful mission in Jesus, the Christ.

Where do we find the God who calls us to peace and to justice as the basis of peace? He tells us very clearly that we find him in his little ones, and especially in one another.

What is distinctive about religious life is not that religious live the counsels, which actually are meant for all Christians, but that they take upon themselves to live these radically in community for the kingdom of God. If they are not merely to observe their vows, but to use them for the kingdom and its values of human dignity, peace, freedom and justice, they must be nurtured by community and in turn nurture community. The universalization of love and the ultimate aim of the counsels will be realized as we enter deeply into religious community. As the Church is called to be light, leaven, salt for the world and to reach out as servant of all, so religious called as they are to be to the Church what the Church is to be to the world have to lead the way in establishing true fellowship with all men and women. They above all cannot allow any segment of humanity to be wiped out of the circle of human beings through the nicknames or epithets that make things out of persons. The "gooks" of the Vietnam War, the "commies" of Nicaragua, in the parlance of the United States today, are signs of a real lack of understanding of the basic message of Christianity. If ever our nation needed leadership in loving, loving even our enemies, it is today. Unless we can show genuine love to the Russians, the Cubans and the others whom we consider enemies, we can never call the Church itself to a Christian way of life in today's world.

No genuine Christian can look upon himself as the saved, the good, and the others as bad and damned. It is only a truly interdependent person, one who has found God in brother and sister, one who lives fellowship in its deepest reality, that can reach out to all without distinction.

A man who has become a familiar figure to many of us through his martyrdom is Oscar Romero, archbishop of San Salvador. Archbishop Romero, though not a member of a religious community, eventually came to live in genuine fellowship with his co-workers. In his own life there was evident a dramatic response to God's grace calling him not merely to work for the people he served, as he had done faithfully all his priestly life, but gradually to come to work with them, and finally as one of them. I saw him in those final days of his life when he had come to be truly one of his people. Although always kind, generous and apostolic in his service of the people, he was doing all this at a certain distance. One day after he was appointed to the see of San Salvador, he was making the rounds of the towns of the archdiocese. In one village a family came and offered him half of a tomato. The archbishop was hurt by this seeming slight. He did not show this to the people, but one of his priests noticed it in him and quietly explained to him what had actually taken place. This was one half of all that family had to eat that day, and they wanted to share with him as an act of their esteem. The archbishop was stunned by this reality. He came to see what it meant to be working not just for, but with the people, and to understand more deeply their situation and their basic needs. From then on he was truly on their side in the work of justice. And as he grew in his love and relationship to the people, he gradually became one of them. They were able to call him by a name of deepest Christian significance, El Compañero, the one who eats bread with us. I understood this the very morning of his assassination. He had arranged for a group of us to meet with the refugees that he was befriending there in San Salvador. After hearing the stories of the refugees, and how they had to risk torture and death in order to flee to the capital, we asked them how they found the courage to do this. Their only answer was "El Compañero"—the archbishop. They knew and fully trusted that he would do everything possible for them. He was truly one of them. And he was true to his word. That day he gave his life for them, snatched from him by a bullet aimed at the heart of Jesus the Christ, who would tell these people that they were worth dying for. Archbishop Romero found God in the fellowship of the peasant refugees and they found Jesus, the Christ most genuinely in the heart of a man who became one of them in Christian fellowship.

We as American religious have to rediscover this basic truth that salvation is not merely individual, but communal. And for each of us a primary community is absolutely necessary for any true response to the Gospel. It may be unrealistic to expect that all primary relationships be formed within the single group of a local community, and we should not load a religious community with the whole responsibility for the satisfaction of its member's needs.[2] However, if one does not find a primary community somewhere within his or her religious community, there is serious doubt that such will be found satisfactorily outside the community. If we approach other groups from a position of weakness we are asking too much of them. This holds true of anyone accepting the gift of a celibate life. Among diocesan clergy there is a great need for deep friendship of fellow priests, a primary community providing a base for further deep friendships. One diocesan priest was reflecting on his own experience of this. He mentioned that he had a primary community with a family of the parish. Every Sunday after Mass and at other times he would be with them. One Sunday afternoon the wife turned to him in the presence of her husband and said "Father Joe, you are as close to me as Jim." The priest realized very clearly then that he was asking more of this family unit than they could possibly give. He needed the fellowship of his priest friends vowed to the same life.

The ministries within a primary community, ministries of awakening of healing and of challenge, are needed by all of us, particularly by major superiors who may easily slip into isolation from their brothers. Awakening one to his full potential at times of change in the patterns of one's life, at times when one's worth is questioned because of certain failures or new challenges. Healing from the hurts that affect us all, but that go so deeply in one who is lonely. Challenging when

---

2. Gregory Many, "Realistic Community Expectations," *Human Development,* Summer 1981; Evelyn M. Woodward, "Uses of Power in Community," *Human Development,* Summer 1983.

one desperately needs a word from a brother who has already proven his genuine love through the other ministries of awakening and of healing. It is in such ministry that the presence of God is experienced. He is clearly seen in the concern of a real brother for one in need. Communal prayer, faith sharing, yes even recreation can all enhance the relationship, the fellowship that mediates the experience of God. And through this, superiors may all take the journey of Archbishop Romero, to work not merely for but with and finally as one of the brothers.

As we come to experience God in our own communities, it becomes so much easier to accept the New Testament reality that Jesus the Christ is actually among us to the extent that even the prayers of petition of a truly Christian community are addressed to the members of that community. How is this possible? The God who answers prayers is the God who is in Christ, who is in the community. This mysterious identification of Christ with the Christian community is a major theme in Matthew because the whole Gospel is bracketed by the two affirmations, "Behold, a virgin shall conceive and bear a son, and his name shall be called Emmanuel, which means 'God with us' " (1:23) and "All authority in heaven and on earth has been given to me. Go, therefore, and make disciples of all nations . . . teaching them to observe all that I have commanded; and behold, I am with you always, to the close of the age" (28:18-20). Precisely the same idea is enunciated in Christ's question to Paul on the Damascus road, "Saul, Saul, why do you persecute me?" (Acts 9:4), because Christ says "me" rather than "mine," even though Paul was in fact persecuting the Christian community. It is this God with us who answers prayers. In a genuine community, a fellowship, the needs of one automatically become an obligation for others. "In answering prayers God preserves the incarnational mode inaugurated by the sending of his Son. If prayers are answered, it is we in fellowship who answer them. This is not to say that the only way in which God can act is through the Christian community. Miracles can happen, and there are no limits on God's mode of acting. However, if we recognize the authority of the New Testament, we must admit that the normal mode of God's response is the incarnational one."[3]

---

3. Jerome Murphy O'Connor, O.P., "What Is Religious Life? Ask the Scriptures."

When we do find God in our primary communities and in the broader fellowship of a religious province or congregation, we find him in the Church and in the world. I have been privileged to visit Nicaragua a number of times these last years, going both during the time of Somoza and after the revolution. I remember one very dedicated religious sister who had served the people during the trying times of Somoza. She had done everything possible to alleviate their hunger and want. After the revolution the state honored her with the title "heroine" of the revolution. I met her shortly after the fighting had ceased and asked her what she was doing. This religious woman, who had learned genuine community in her congregation and had found God in the fellowship of her sisters, told me that after the revolution she had prayed, asking God what he wanted of her now. And the answer she received was startling. "He wanted me on the other side." She knew that she was to go to serve those who were now in prison for the terrible crimes committed during the war. Since there was no capital punishment allowed, all of those captured were now held in prisons. She volunteered to work with the human rights commission to protect the rights of these prisoners. And she went to one woman, who had lost a boy in the fighting, and who had one of her daughters terribly maltreated in prison, and another who had lost both hands. She asked the woman if she would really forgive those who had done such horrible things, and if she were willing to come and serve them now in prison. Her answer was "yes." She did forgive and she would come. A father who had lost two boys in the fighting also volunteered to come with them. Day after day they are at the prisons, seeing that no one mistreats the prisoners, and that their needs are met. Fellowship . . . community, even with one's worst enemies.

As we look at our apostolates in the United States we realize how much we need the experience of God in fellowship and ask how we might help our people toward such an experience. The United States Catholic desperately needs genuine community. Many of the sects are taking our people, people that look for community in Church. Can our parishes become such communities? Not unless the smaller units, families, basic communities of neighborhoods, etc., experience the reality of fellowship within themselves. And who can call them to this, if not a religious community, coming from different backgrounds, united not by any bond of family or race, but forming in Christ's name a giving, nurturing community, fellowship?[4] If we have found him there, we are ready to share. Every gift received is meant to be given.

Thomas E. Clarke, S.J.
OUR SEARCH FOR GOD IN SOLITUDE

Not many miles from this campus, almost a century and a half ago, that famous Yankee, Henry Thoreau, wrote about his cabin by Walden Pond. He said that he had three chairs in the cabin, one for solitude, one for friendship, and one for society.

Each of our days here at Boston College has given us experience of each of these three aspects of our humanity—we have had time to be alone, time for our group and for informal sharing with just a few, and time all together, in this auditorium and in St. Ignatius Church, for a larger societal experience of being Church in the world.

This morning we reflect together on the dimension of *solitude* in our integral experience of being human, being Christian, being religious.

When I first heard the theme of this talk, I thought of Henri Nouwen—and William McNamara, and the Baroness de Hueck, and Ed Farrell, and Ruth Burrows—and Charles de Foucauld and Teresa of Avila and St. Augustine. And I said to myself, "What can I possibly say to major superiors about solitude that they haven't heard or read over and over again, from people who have had much more experience of solitude than I have had?"

But then I realized that the planning group for this Assembly wanted to highlight the linkage between the search for God in solitude, in fellowship, and in the world. What would it be like, I asked myself, to explore the search for God in solitude while paying special attention to some aspects of this linkage?

And so this reflection on solitude begins with a major assumption: that for us today the societal and cultural context of the inner search is *apocalyptic* in character. If this assumption is correct, then I believe that our exercise of solitude must be characterized, first by a readiness for conflict, second by an awareness that transcendent powers of good

---

4. I would propose the statement of Leonardo Boff in his book *God's Witnesses in the Heart of the World:* "The specific charism of religious life is to explicate the experience of God in Jesus Christ, lived in fellowship, expressed by public consecration, introduced into the world as a prophetic sign of the future of the world."

and evil are locked in combat within the human spirit, and third by the conviction that the principal weapons of our spiritual warfare have to do with myth and symbol, with the play of imagination and the passionate working of the human heart. These three characteristics—readiness for struggle, acknowledgment of the conflict of transcendent good and evil, and the engagement of the mythic and symbolic imagination and passions of the heart—are familiar to us as Christians especially through that very last book of the Bible, whose time has come again in our day—the Book of Revelation.

What is being trivialized this summer in escapist fashion in the *Return of the Jedi* and in the game rooms of our shopping malls and airports, what children and artists and the emotionally troubled perceive with their sensitive antennae, is in fact the struggle for humanity itself, and, in Christian perspective, the overthrow of the kingdom of Satan by the coming kingdom of God, manifested in Christ Jesus and proclaimed by the Church. Any search for God in solitude by an ecclesial leader in today's world and today's Church which does not place itself within such an apocalyptic context would, in my opinion, be escapist and irresponsible. This may appear to be a grim appraisal of what is, in its totality, a call to joy and peace and victory, but I believe it to be an inescapable analysis. We live in the midst of apocalypse, and our solitude needs to acknowledge it.

What does it mean to search for God in solitude? As Alan McCoy has said, our discovery of God is always mediated by some created reality. In search for God in solitude the medium is the unique self that I am and can become. The search for God in this dimension is the search for the true self, for authentic personhood, for God's image within as constitutive of my deepest being. Dynamically conceived, solitude is the lifelong journey from the initial image of God toward the fullness of likeness to God. *Redeam ad me, redeam ad te,* Augustine prayed. The journey to and through the real self is the journey to God.

Being a human journey, the search for God in solitude will always be both *cognitive* and *affective,* a road of *truth* and a road of *freedom.* At a moment of history that is apocalyptic in character, solitude will be marked by special qualities which I would now like to describe.

"You shall know the truth." Cognitively, Christian solitude is a struggle for truth and fidelity in the face of illusion, deception, hypocrisy. Within each of us is the Spirit of truth, the Spirit of the One who said, "I am the Truth." But also within us, if we are honest, lives another spirit, begotten by the father of lies, by the one who was a liar from the beginning. In solitude, within each of us, this struggle for truth takes place.

And it takes place in two contexts, secular and ecclesiastical. Its secular context is a culture where the nobility of truth still lives, a society still capable, at its best, of naming the ugly monsters of racism and sexism, militarism and abortionism, for what they are. But it is also a society inundated with untruth, through the massive manipulation of people's hopes and fears, images and feelings, in the interest of economic and political aggrandizement. This flood of institutionalized and acculturated deception today threatens progressively to mesmerize people, to blunt their critical powers, to paralyze their God-given capacity to discern between what is true and what is false. The search for God in solitude today, then, needs to be a vigilant and passionate effort not to be taken in, not to let one's critical perception be numbed by the ingrained untruth of a culture in the grip of the father of lies. Positively, it needs to be discipleship to the one who said, "Let your speech be 'Yea, Yea' and 'Nay, Nay,' " the one who said to Pilate, "For this was I born, for this have I come into the world, that I might bear witness to the truth." Just a few months ago, our U.S. bishops gave us a courageous example of witnessing to truth when they testified to the naked emperor of technological militarism. Out of what search for God in solitude, we may ask, did this brave witness emerge, especially on the part of the initial small group of so called "peace bishops"? And what is the power for truth that can be released in our country in coming months and years if our search for God in solitude is a journey of truth?

The *ecclesiastical* context of the search in solitude for truth is quite different, especially for those who exercise power and office in the institutional Church. Here the principal enemy of truth for clerics in general is a bland cynicism, evasiveness, passivity, which, like the priest and the Levite on the road to Jericho, would rather not notice the ugly wounds that disfigure the Church or any part of it. There is possibly no more critical and painful point of personal discernment in the life of a bishop or major superior than to be faced with the question of societal truth, the question of whether, especially by silence, he may be acquiescing in some major untruth within the body of Christ. The forms of such temptations can be varied. They may touch the domestic life of your community, or they may have to do with how your community and other communities relate to the larger institutional Church, particularly when laws and procedures affront human dignity. Though the witness you may be asked to render to truth in such instances is public in character, and though fellowship in rendering that witness is crucial, it is also in solitude that each one is confronted with the requirement of truth. It is in solitude that the simplicity and the clarity and the courage to be faithful to the truth will be given if we seek it as the gift that it is. I would guess that your statement on clericalism which you are sharing with the members of your communities could not have been possible unless a number of you in solitude and fellowship had first permitted difficult questions about clericalism to emerge.

Besides truth, the search for God in solitude is a search for the *freedom* befitting the children of God. The two values are, of course, intertwined. "You shall know the truth, and the truth shall make you free." "Where the Spirit of God is, there is freedom." "It was for freedom," Paul tells the Galatians, "that Christ has set you free."

One of the major gains of theology in recent decades has been to recapture an understanding of Christian freedom, as distinct from the *liberum arbitrium* or free will of philosophical discourse, which for centuries had overshadowed the freedom of which Jesus and Paul and Augustine spoke. This is the freedom with which God is free, manifested in the heroic human freedom of Jesus Christ, and made available to all through the gift of the Spirit. God, who always does what he wants to do, wishes to bestow on us the freedom to do and become what we really want to do and become. Paul speaks of this freedom in Romans 8, and in chapter 7 he speaks of the unfreedom which is the very heart of the sinful human condition: I find myself not doing what I really want, and doing what I really don't want.

The search for God in solitude is the struggle to grow in the exercise of this gift of freedom, in the practice of doing what we really want, in the face of all those forces, within and without, which would keep us enslaved. In this aspect too, the search for God in solitude is apocalyptic in its context. As illusion and cynicism are the enemies of truth, so addiction and subservience are the enemies of freedom, emerging respectively from the contexts of secular culture and ecclesiastical institution.

As secular this struggle is with the massive addictiveness which our culture tends to induce in people, individually, in groups, and en masse. Closely linked with illusion and fantasy, addiction in a myriad of forms keeps people from being free, from doing what they really want. A nation of automatons, marionettes, is the logical outcome of what is happening to human freedom in today's technological culture. The underlying ideology of the market economy requires a giant pool of consumers obedient to the identification of their needs by the very forces which profit from the mindless inflation of those needs. The calculated cultivation of consumerism keeps people so hooked on commodities that they acquiesce in being themselves treated as commodities. In commercialism's own "marvelous exchange," as John Kavanaugh has noted, products are given the status of persons as persons are transformed into products, into mere things. And this squandering of the gifts of nature and of precious human energies not only takes place at the expense of the poor of the world, but dehumanizes its unwitting immediate victims, middle class America.

What is most ominous about this erosion of freedom through the media today is the extension of marketing techniques from the sale of material goods to the sale of political policies, parties, candidates, and even values. A fully automated electorate is not unimaginable. 1984 is less than five months away.

It is in the face of this assault on freedom from the culture of technologism that the exercise of Christian freedom in solitude takes on a character unknown to other ages of Christian contemplation. For now alternative, non-addictive, truly free exercise of the gifts of imagination and feeling in genuine contemplation and leisure becomes both a personal and a societal imperative. The Book of Revelation, Ephesians and Colossians, Deutero-Isaiah and other prophetic books offer us models and a stimulus for an energetic dreaming hope which can redeem us from the addictiveness which surrounds us. We are not condemned to being playthings of the marketplace. We can be free citizens capable of making a difference, restoring health to—yes, a sick society.

How shall we name the ecclesiastical threat to freedom, and the appropriate response in solitude to that threat? Were I speaking to a group of alienated Catholics, on the periphery of the institutional Church, my response would be quite different. But for leaders of the institutional Church in the United States almost two decades after Vatican II's *Declaration on Religious Freedom,* the primary threat remains a feudal, anti-modern authoritarianism which still blocks the

full acceptance within the Church of those principles of religious freedom which the Council affirmed for secular society. As Heinz
Schlette writes in *Sacramentum Mundi*, ". . . the seriousness of the
Council's statements with regard to religious liberty . . . will be mea-
sured by the readiness of the Church itself to allow room for 'religious
freedom' within its own walls. . . . If in the concrete life of the
Church . . . all of its members cannot be truly free, free from fear,
suspicion and supervision . . . the Church in its role of advocate of
social and civil liberties would have to remain suspect."[5]

Admittedly religious freedom within the Church, human and
Christian rights for all the baptized, is a societal issue, to be dealt with
primarily in the critique and reform of Church structures and institutions. But what, I would ask would be the quality of a solitude into
which the issue of ecclesial freedom did not enter as a crucial question
of conscience? In addition, it is in contemplative solitude that each of
us needs to experience most deeply that freedom before God which is
the paradigm and mainstay of our interpersonal and societal freedom
in the Church. In proportion as we experience God's commands as
liberating, God's law—the inner law of the life-giving Spirit—as a call
not to subservience but to freedom, we come forth from solitude convinced that the holy name of our divine Creator and lover of our freedom must never be invoked for any form, secular or ecclesiastical, of
the denial of human dignity and freedom.

Before concluding, two further remarks may clarify what I have
said, and what I have not said. First, I have spoken of the search for
God in solitude in a way which links it closely with the search for God
in the world. I have not spoken about the way in which the values of
truth and freedom in fellowship, in human relationships, influence
and are influenced by the search for God in solitude. Some of you may
wish to reflect on this linkage of solitude and fellowship.

Second, in this sketch of how the struggle for truth and freedom
in solitude within an apocalyptic context might be conceived, I have
almost necessarily, I'm afraid, conveyed the impression that our solitude must be primarily employed in problem solving. I do not believe
that. On the contrary I believe that the major exercise of solitude
needs to be contemplative rather than reflective or elective. The un-

---

5. Volume 5, page 297.

pragmatic play of images, together with the grateful retrieval of rev-
elatory moments of one's personal story, is in the long run far more
crucial for truthful and free choices of conscience than the weighing
of rational pros and cons. And "the sweet doing of nothing" in prayer
and other forms of leisure is, in a society tyrannized by the work ethic,
a most powerful countercultural agent.

Ultimately it is only persons transfigured by dwelling contempla-
tively with myth and symbol and silence and the mysterious "reasons
of the heart" who will be capable of emerging from the castle or the
cave with the stamina to lead the struggle with the powers of darkness.
But unless solitude in its contemplative aspect is joined, through the
values of truth and freedom, to this apocalyptic moment of secular and
ecclesiastical history, it will be a sterile escape from our mission to the
world.

In conclusion, let me say a brief and pragmatic word about how
this model of the search for God in solitude relates to the vowed life
and to your role as leaders. In the coming months you will be engaged
in helping your membership and also our U.S. bishops in a reflection
on the meaning and shape of the vowed apostolic life. The caliber of
those named to the episcopal commission, the committee of religious
and the role of consultants, gives promise of a fruitful dialogue. I think
it follows from all that I have said today that a truthful and free naming of issues and raising of doubts is essential if this process is to be
marked with integrity. Some of the language employed in the document from SCRIS and even in the new law of the Church regarding
apostolic religious life raises serious questions for many apostolic religious in the United States. Is the charismatic apostolic life that we
have chosen appropriately described, for example, through the language of separation from the world? Is it fully accurate to say that "the
first and principal duty of apostolic religious is assiduous union with
God in prayer"?[6] What is to be said in an American context of the
proportionate attention and emphasis given in both documents to the
authority of general chapters as compared with the authority of individual superiors? Though the dialogue on these and similar questions
will be a dialogue in fellowship dealing in large part with institutional

6. "Essential Elements in Church Teaching on Religious Life," n. 26 (*Origins*, July 7, 1983), p. 141.

reality, its success quite clearly needs to engage the search for God in solitude on the part of all. It is a holy journey that we make with one another, in the Church, and for the world. May we learn to walk in truth and in freedom. "You shall know the truth, and the truth shall make you free."[7]

---

7. Limitations of time have unfortunately made it impossible to include some reflections on personal, interpersonal and societal impasse, based on a powerful paper by Sister Constance Fitzgerald, O.C.D. The paper will be published in a volume, *Living With Apocalypse: Resources for Compassion*, edited by Tilden Edwards, and to be published by Harper & Row, Spring 1984.

TRENDS IN RELIGIOUS LIFE TODAY

John M. Lozano, C.M.F.

The following article is the only one in this volume not originally prepared for the Conference of Major Superiors of Men. We include it here because it provides a significant summary of trends in religious life in the United States today and is very much in line with the evolving leadership of both Conferences of Major Superiors.

The author is a specialist in the theology of religious life and a professor at the Catholic Theological Union in Chicago. His book *Discipleship: Towards an Understanding of Religious Life* (Chicago: Claret Center, 1980) has been much appreciated by American religious.

This essay originally appeared in *Review for Religious,* Vol. 42, pp. 481–505 (July/August, 1983). It is reprinted here with permission.

The following reflections are offered as a sort of aerial photograph of the most prominent features emerging on the landscape of the religious life. We will take a look at some of the main trends that seem to be shaping the future of this landscape and examine some of the main difficulties that its terrain presents for the religious traveler today. Many of these trends and difficulties seem to be closely interrelated. At the end of our survey we will concentrate on one major difficulty that seems to arise from causes that are more general than is sometimes supposed.

I will be speaking mainly from the viewpoint of the northern hemisphere (North America and Europe), but my work in some other parts of the globe (Latin America, Australia and the Philippines) has shown that the same trends are emerging in broad areas throughout the Church. The rapidity of modern communications and the international outreach of books and reviews has tended to hasten the spread of ideas and attitudes from one continent to another.

I base these reflections on my personal experience. During the last twenty years, which I have dedicated to studying the religious life and working with a broad spectrum of men's and women's religious communities, I have always striven to relate a theological vision of the religious life to the experiences that I and those I worked with were undergoing at the time. I have also had to pay close attention to what others were writing on these subjects. Naturally, my nearness to the phenomena I deal with (my own present) has been a somewhat mixed blessing; on the one hand, it has given me the immediacy of an "insider's" experience of these phenomena; on the other, it has been a real test of objectivity, since I had to write about them with a degree of passionate involvement. For this is a history we are all enjoying and suffering together.

In the exposition that follows, I have chosen not to separate trends in theology from trends in life, since common sense and all my previous work have shown them to be intimately related.

A PRELIMINARY OBSERVATION: THE CRISIS OF RELIGIOUS LIFE

There is no need to dwell on the particular circumstances that lead us to reflect on the present state of the religious life. It is a well-known fact that religious life is currently undergoing a serious crisis of growth and adaptation. Many are wondering if it really has a future,[1] while a number of communities who have experienced a sharp decline in membership are worrying whether they will manage to survive. It makes little sense to try to lay the blame on individual failures. We must remember that individuals tend to withdraw from institutions when institutions lose their meaning. What we are going through is a failure of institutions as such.[2] In general, these crises in institutions of religious life have come at a time when civil society is undergoing a crisis which, in turn, affects the Church on a deep level. This is not surprising if we bear in mind the profound technological and cultural changes that have taken place in our society, as well as the rapidity with which they have occurred and will continue to occur. The Second Vatican Council spoke of our times as a new epoch in history and tried to make the Church face up to it. In a memorable address to the Weston School of Theology, Karl Rahner stated that the "Second Vatican Council is, in a rudimentary form, still groping for identity, the Church's first self-actualization as a World Church."[3] Thus the third great epoch of the Church's history is beginning to open up, after the very brief Judeo-Christian epoch and the Occidental epoch that started when Paul brought the Gospel to the Gentiles and began incarnating it in their culture. The deep changes which this new epoch will bring, although they will surely be of great consequence for the Church, can as yet hardly be glimpsed.

If the Church is already witnessing some of these profound changes, then the religious life, which in its various forms has always tried to respond to the needs of the Church, will itself have to undergo a necessary crisis of readjustment. That is why we simply have to reflect on what is going on.

We must, nevertheless, emphasize that the term "crisis" does not have an exclusively negative denotation. In the past, crises in institutions of religious life have always been the crucible in which new forms and new families have taken shape. It will be sufficient to recall what happened in the sixth (the Master, Benedict), twelfth (Cistercians, Canons Regular), thirteenth (mendicants) and sixteenth centuries (apostolic institutes).

Because we are still in the middle of a crisis, and because critical periods seem to be those in which the Holy Spirit is especially at work, we simply have to reflect on what is occurring.

In dealing with the most general trends observable in the religious life today, it seemed appropriate to group them under the following six headings: (1) the centrality of the person, (2) the growing advocacy of women's rights, (3) the predominance of life over institutions, (4) ministerial openness to the world, (5) the reinterpretation of religious life, and (6) the problem of lifelong commitment. Finally, we will consider a single issue of great concern: the scarcity of vocations.

1. THE CENTRALITY OF THE PERSON

The frequency with which certain aspects of religious life are discussed, and the way in which certain concrete situations are handled, reveal a growing tendency to regard the religious person as a central criterion. This theme has been the object of deep philosophical reflection by Christian thinkers during our century. In France, it was first dealt with by Jacques Maritain and then in a quite different way by Emmanuel Mounier. In Europe generally, the trauma of modern dictatorships—which made party or national loyalty the life-or-death criterion for the individual—also helped us see the dangers latent in the way some religious families viewed issues of solidarity and obedience. The trauma was a salutary one, because both the theoretical authoritarianism of anti-democrats like Charles Maurras and the practical authoritarianism of dictators like Mussolini, Salazar, Franco and Peron had no small influence in some ecclesiastical and religious circles. But since the time of John XXIII, a new definition of the common good has begun to leave its mark on magisterial teachings and statements.[4] This definition regards the common good not as the sum of common goals (to which individuals are sacrificed), but as an environment of freedom, peace and solidarity where persons may more readily achieve development and fulfillment. Even in the darkest hours of the past, no matter how much we conformed, somewhere in the back of our memory we could never quite let go of the Lord's saying that "the sabbath was made for human beings, not human beings for the sabbath," or of the pastoral axiom that "the sacaraments are for persons." But clearly, our more democratic milieu and the institutional images it projects, together with the spread of the new psychologies of personal development in Europe and North America, have made us more sensitive to this theme.

1.1. *The Development of One's Own Talents.* This is not only an important concern for individual religious, but also figures in a whole series of renewed constitutions. In the past, constitutions ordinarily asked community leaders to watch over the spiritual and physical welfare of their sisters and brothers.[5] The new texts ask them to facilitate the overall growth of their sisters and brothers, whether on the level of psychological health, education or professional preparation.[6] In fact, a number of the new constitutions speak of the overall growth of the religious and make the community co-responsible with the individual in achieving this growth.[7] The now-common secretariats and programs for continuing formation and education point in the same direction.

But individual religious share this concern. There is a general tendency to affirm oneself and develop one's gifts. This has had its effect on spirituality, which is viewed as a means for achieving one's full potential (holiness/wholeness), and on the theology of the vows, which are viewed dynamically, as means to personal growth.[8] The achievement of personal fulfillment was already a goal in the teaching of Aquinas and Bonaventure, who treated the vows as means for arriving at the perfection of charity,[9] although greater stress is laid today on the overall aspect of maturity.

Some studies on the types of candidates who are seeking to enter religious life reveal not only that generally they show a visible concern for their personal growth (a legitimate concern), but also that they tend to manifest a certain self-centeredness and at the same time expect much support from the community. This phenomenon is obviously not a reaction to the earlier stress on communal goals in the religious institutes, since we are talking about new candidates, untouched by those experiences. Members of boards of admissions should try to understand, with the help of psychologists, the reasons for this attitude and its intensity, since it may denote a certain frailty in the applicant. For most of these candidates a healthy community life can have a therapeutic function. We are convinced that in the future, even more than in the past, a healthy community life (spiritual ambiance, interpersonal relationships, mutual concern and support) will be the main condition for the survival of religious (individuals and institutions). The future of religious life is in the hands of the formation directors.

1.2. *Individual Growth and Solidarity.* One difficulty felt by many religious and frequently echoed in religious chapters and congresses can be summed up in the question: How are one's personal fulfillment and gifts to be related to the common good, aims and ministries of the institute?[10] Theoretically, the issue seems clear enough. On the one hand, the members of every religious community share a common vocation and have received from God the same charism that was first given to their founder or foundress. On the other hand, each member is a different personality, with different gifts that he or she has a duty to cultivate and make bear fruit. In short, it is a matter of a diversity of personalities being united in communion. We should perhaps note in passing that actual, absolute liberty, that is, the real possibility of developing one's personality to the maximum, simply does not exist. Every adult, even one who is single and free, has to build his or her existence within a limited gamut of possibilities, and always with some attendant sacrifices. No one, let alone a person committed to one or more persons in a family, in matrimony or in a celibate community, can work out his or her own development without reference to solidarity to others. Anyone who persists in trying to evade solidarity will end up psychologically warped or stunted. Individual religious must always be ready to make sacrifices, and these sacrifices will definitely make them grow. However, on its part, the community cannot pursue its common good or goals through a systematic policy of sacrificing its members. The development and happiness of individual members carries over into the common good of the group. The concrete solution to this problem is to be sought and found in a sense of communion and real dialogue between the group (its representatives) and the individual.

1.3. *Freedom.* Isaac Hecker, with fine American sense, wrote that "a great and large freedom of action should be the spirit" of the Paulist community.[11] It is significant that the terms "freedom" and "liberty" occur so frequently in revised constitutions.[12] Of course, individual freedom of choice has always been required for acceptance into community. One was—and is—in community, out of a desire to be in community. But community and obedience were commonly seen from the viewpoint of sacrificing one's individual freedom. In the new type of community there is ample room for individual freedom and initiative. We have referred in passing to the disappearance of the disciplinary type of community that began forming in the nineteenth century, with its peculiar stresses in reaction to the French Revolution: a type of community dominated by uniformity in dress, in timetables and, in lay communities of women and men, in the kind of ministry practiced. The new constitutions contain few disciplinary regulations. The local community can now, ordinarily, determine its own internal norms and make its own decisions. The number of community acts, which were excessive in many communities founded in the last few centuries, has been reduced to a minimum. Not only religious men, but religious women as well, now have to seek out their own ministerial works, rather than receive them passively from the community. Recently a sister told me: "We ourselves have to create our own jobs and living conditions." Obviously, this kind of freedom has its price. A religious must now make a real effort to maintain communion with his or her own group. Today's community tends to be seen in the light of unity in essentials, liberty in what does not affect the common values of religious life or the charism and spirit of the institute, and a definite effort at establishing a communion of love.

Initially, the downfall of restrictive norms and community acts, together with the broadening field for autonomous, individual decisions, left a good number of religious with the impression that community life had all but disappeared. However, after a period of personal search, religious began to feel the need to return to a more intensely lived form of community, this time based on interpersonal relationships. More spontaneous and creative acts of common prayer began to appear. Nevertheless, there are quite a few men and women religious who have kept their liberty without managing to create communion. Of course, many religious live in community, in the sense that they come home to sleep under the same roof, share meals together and treat each other with respect. But the number of religious who are living alone, when they could be living in community, is somewhat notable. The fact that more women than men are living alone may be traced to a number of factors. For one thing, the number of men whose work is tied to institutions (parishes, schools, retreat houses) is proportionately greater. Moreover, women religious may have a greater psychological need for living alone. In the past, women's communities were far more restrictive than men's, and thus the reaction of the former has been that much stronger. Besides this, as we shall see in more detail later, all women, and religious women in particular, are struggling to emerge as persons, against the restrictions still imposed on them by the ecclesiastical community.

1.4. *Pluralism in Community.* This brings us to the subject of pluralism, which was so warmly debated in not a few chapters of renewal. In the past, there was a strong tendency toward uniformity. Everyone studied the same theology and followed the same methods of prayer. Each institute had a uniform theological or spiritual language. Today the great variety of theological positions in the Church is reflected within religious families, and often within the same religious house. This affects the way we view the religious life and its objectives, and these different views are translated into different life-styles.

Pluralism can immensely enrich our communities, provided it does not jeopardize essentials, thus weakening or undermining spiritual cohesion. But pluralism has now reached a transitional phase in which it can give rise to considerable suffering. Those who are inclined toward a more traditional type of life, to a distinctive habit, or to a more devotional form of piety may suffer and feel lost among others who are leading a different type of life. Those who are inclined to a more personal life-style, with a more modern sensibility, often feel that they are the object of suspicion and insinuations. Theological pluralism, above all for initiates, can cause acute moral suffering. We may sometimes be offered an image of Christ, or a paradigm for relationships with Christ, that wounds our feelings.

We might do well to recall that pluralism in freedom caused serious problems for the tiny ecclesial communities of Paul, both on the theological level (the role of the law) and on the practical level (eating food offered to idols). Paul's recommendation was that all should practice a delicate charity toward one another. Those who felt more restricted should respect the conscience of others, while those who felt more free in these matters should exercise their freedom without inflicting unnecessary wounds on those of a different persuasion. "Each of you should regard, not your own interests, but the other person's" (1 Cor 10:24). There are religious who worry too much about what others are saying or doing. And there are religious who speak and act without regard for the sufferings they may be causing others. After all, what good will our theology or our achievement of practical freedom do us if they are done without love?

1.5. *Personal Ministries*. In the past, congregations with the most priests practiced two different types of ministries: one, institutional, in which the religious collaborated in a common work (schools, retreat houses, parishes), the other, personal (teaching in centers outside the institute, preaching, conferences, books). Lay communities of men or women were limited to working within their own institutions (hospitals, schools). In many women's communities and in some brothers' institutes, there is now a trend favoring personal ministries: counseling, spiritual direction and giving conferences. This has fundamentally modified the type of community life led in these institutes. We read also, for example, that the Franciscan Province of Santa Barbara has adopted, as a criterion of priority in assignments to ministries, the talents and availability of individual members, rather than the needs of existing institutions.[13] This trend can be noted with lesser force in institutes that have a greater number of institutions (schools, parishes, hospitals).

1.6. *Emphasis on Local Community*. Partly because of this affirmation of the centrality of the person in societies and institutions, and partly because of the current stress on the Church as a communion that is realized above all in the local church, greater importance is being attached to the local religious community. Many constitutions have changed the vertical presentation of their governmental structures from the once-common descending order (general government, provinces, local communities) to an ascending order (local, provincial, general),[14] while even more constitutions affirm the primary value of the local community. In contrast with the mainly disciplinary content of former texts, the new ones bring out the theological and ecclesial meaning of the local community as a community of faith, worship and mission, and as the privileged *locus* of Christian communion.[15]

1.7. *Small Communities.* Starting very soon after the Council, there was a growing emphasis on a trend that had already appeared in religious institutes founded a few decades earlier: the formation of small local communities with a family-like structure. Large communities that staffed various institutions (schools or parishes), or were at the service of some large institution (a university), began dividing up into small groups. Many factors motivated this shift: a desire to establish closer interpersonal relationships, an attempt to lessen the difficulties inherent in large-group interaction, a tendency to live closer to the people, and an endeavor to free the group from quasi-monastic structures. Paul VI dealt with this trend in his apostolic exhortation, *Evangelica Testificatio*,[16] noting that this type of community makes greater demands of its members. For one thing, in this setting the individual constantly emerges in face-to-face relationships that strongly reveal his or her good points and shortcomings. Small communities demand better communication, greater respect for individual differences, and a more thoroughgoing effort to adapt oneself to others. In large communities it is easier to avoid communication and, above all, confrontation with certain community members. Interestingly enough, it is not just older persons accustomed to a more institutionalized type of life, but also younger religious less inclined to intimate communication, who prefer to live in larger groups.

1.8. *Authority and Obedience.* The Second Vatican Council, in its decree *Perfectae Caritatis*,[17] clearly established principles for a deep renewal of the practice of authority and obedience as we had heretofore known it. Doubtless, the concepts expressed in this decree belong to the tradition of religious life in its richest moments. Nevertheless, the emphasis on certain aspects of this tradition, such as "active collaboration," the service rendered by the community leader, the recommendation that the leader respect his or her fellow religious as sons or daughters of God and as human persons, the insistence on dialogue as an integral part of the unifying process of obedience (and not just as a last resort in facing difficult decisions)—all of these paved the way for a theological and practical reinterpretation of the leader's role, and of the nature of common obedience.[18] Even those institutes that have not modified their vertical structures of government have had to re-read their constitutions with a new sensitivity.[19] The Council stated that the manner of governing religious institutes had to be examined and brought into harmony with the physical and psychological conditions of today's religious, with the needs of the apostolate, with cultural requirements, and with socio-economic realities.[20] The great majority of the revised constitutions of institutes, founded in an age when another image of authority prevailed, have modified their systems of government by introducing dialogue prior to decision-making, or have even left certain decisions to the group itself. Some constitutions have made the group the ordinary decision-making body in matters important to the local community. In practice, there has also been a tendency to allow a wide margin for individual decisions and initiatives in matters that do not touch upon the life of the group.

Still more recently a certain tendency has emerged to try to put-obedience-back-to-work, by emphasizing almost unilaterally the authority of superiors, the ecclesiastical origin of their power (which may be understood in different ways), and obedience as submission. These statements, which originate from a pastoral concern, must be placed in the larger and richer context of the whole tradition. In this context, obedience is predominately either an attitude of faith in search for God beyond the limitations of the individual (opening oneself to the wisdom and experience of the tradition represented by the leader-monastic obedience), or an expression of mutual love and concern for the group and the individuals (Basilian, Augustinian, mendicant, Ignatian . . . obedience). The sacrifice of our desires and opinions is response to a gift we have received: community. We believe that this more traditional approach is also the best way to help us understand the meaning and value of obedience. We should also notice that group-discernment, expressed in dialogue, is not a paternalistic concession. Even in those cases where the responsibility of the decision is invested in a person, group-discernment is a stage of the process.

2. THE EMANCIPATION OF WOMEN

Closely related to the preceding theme (the value of the person as such), another trend has had a growing impact on religious life: the progressive emergence of the religious woman, and her assumption of a public mission in the Church and in civil society. We are touching here on a painful topic: the struggle of women (and the Holy Spirit with them) to liberate themselves from a situation of confinement and subordination. No need to go into details of Mary Ward's way of the cross, or the fate of the Ursulines after the death of Angela Merici, or the changes forced upon the Order of the Visitation, or the tremendous difficulties that Louise de Marillac and her Daughters of Charity had to face. As late as the nineteenth century, especially in France, every women's institute was forced to have a male ecclesiastical superior with powers equal and sometimes superior to those of the mother general. Some institutes were arbitrarily divided, and some foundresses were practically expelled from their own communities (Clara Pfaender, Bonifacia Rodriguez, Maria Rosa Zangara), or deposed (Jeanne de Lestonnac, Alix Le Clercq, Alfonsa Cavin, Rafaela of the Sacred Heart). Fortunately, circumstances have changed radically and will continue to do so, as we shall see.

2.1. *Emancipation.* A large number of religious women are more or less fully committed to the feminist movement, and still more are deeply affected by it.[21] In the past every religious woman, upon reaching maturity, had to bring her femininity to bear on her milieu so to speak implicitly, by letting it shine through in her life and work (think of Teresa's influence on her theologian friends, or the changes Jeanne de Chantal brought about in Francis de Sales). Nowadays, however, the condition of women is explicitly posited and vindicated. In affirming their identity, religious women are bringing a new dimension into spirituality and religious life in general: the feminine perspective.[22] They not only are setting up a feminine symbology to counterbalance the overstated male symbology of religion (a function always at work in women like Clare of Assisi, Catherine of Siena, Teresa of Jesus and Margaret Mary Alacoque), but are also discovering the feminine aspects of God (something rarely done in the past, although one can always point to the example of Dame Julian of Norwich). The arrival of large numbers of women in the once segregated halls of theology is bound to give rise to deep changes in the task of interpreting the experience of God. The theology of the religious life will surely have to take much more serious note of this phenomenon.

2.2. *The Revision of Constitutions.* Today, religious women are revising their own constitutions, sometimes with the help of outside experts, both men and women. We are getting farther and farther away from the days when men could write rules for women (Pachomius, perhaps Augustine, Caesarius of Arles, Leander), or when women had to adopt and adapt rules written for men's communities (Benedictines). There is an exquisitely feminine style and sensibility in not a few of the new constitutions.

2.3 *Personal Ministries.* With growing frequency, women are taking on personal ministries not connected with their own institutions. They are teaching in outside centers, writing books, doing spiritual direction, directing retreats and spiritual exercises, counseling, ministering in parishes, and so forth. Their influence is beginning to be strongly felt in male formation communities, by the balance they bring to young men who receive their information in an otherwise strictly masculine environment. This gives these men a more positive and educative perception of the feminine image.

2.4. *The First Apostolic Community.* In our judgment, the women religious of North America have built the first fully apostolic feminine community in history. Many of them live in small groups not bound to institutions, and are dedicated to personal ministries. While men religious are frequently tied down to an ecclesiastical institution (parish, college), women religious, by the very fact of being non-ordained ministers, enjoy a greater freedom of movement.

2.5. *Economic Dependence.* This freedom is very relative, however, because many women religious are faced with the anguishing problem of economic dependence. Adding to the painfulness of this situation is the fact that the work they do is usually underpaid. Moreover, those women who do not have their own institutions must either depend on other institutions, or else become free-lancers at the mercy of fortune. A few years ago, one mother general told me that her institute was unable to implement an option for the poor and the marginated because they depended for their sustenance on the salaries they received from the diocese, which did not allow enough for it.

3. LIFE OVER INSTITUTIONS

Another clearly perceptible trend in today's religious life seems to be a distinct prevalence of a concept and an experience of a life lived simply, freely and creatively, over against more institutional forms of living. Significantly, the first schema on religious life submitted to the Second Vatican Council was overloaded with canonical-institutional vocabulary, reflected in its title: *status religiosus*—the religious *state*. It had obviously been drafted by a group of conservative canonists and theologians. When this text was brought to the floor for discussion, the Council gave it a change of direction and chose to speak of the religious *life*, understood not as a sort of entity that could be classified and regulated, but as a life that is really lived. This trend is more apparent in *Perfectae Caritatis* (October 1965) than in Chapter IV of *Lumen Gentium* (November 1964). But even in *Lumen Gentium*, the basis stated for both the religious state and form of life are the charisms of the Spirit,[23] and the movement leading a Christian to consecrate his or her life to the service of God is described in similar terms.[24] *Perfectae Caritatis* describes various concrete aspects of this life which must be renewed and adapted to conditions as they really exist.

This has been a recurring trend throughout history, especially during periods of creativity. Basil and Macrina created fraternal groups, free of the unwieldiness of the Pachomian institutions that had formed in Egypt. Francis of Assisi was very traditional in his concepts of the religious life ("to live according to the Gospel"), yet he launched a project of profound renewal by distancing himself from existing monastic institutions. The Dominicans originally followed this same trend. The first Jesuits and the Daughters of Charity, each in their own way, were simply Christian companions committed to service. A few decades ago, the Little Brothers and Sisters of Jesus returned to this simplicity, to a lived life and to creativity. The phenomenon we have been describing is now appearing under various forms.

3.1. *The Fall of Structure.* In most communities many structures have disappeared. The nineteenth century left us a legacy of methods and detailed regulations for prayer, for the organization of our day, for work, etc. In Europe, a number of founders went so far as to include a basic menu in their constitutions. As the monks of Solesmes had striven to unify liturgical rubrics against a welter of national liturgies, religious superiors strove to unify religious life with regulations and timetables. In today's constitutions and community discussions, the emphasis is on the quality of life. Religious are concerned about the extent to which their real life constitutes a witness, now that neither uniform habits nor characteristic buildings nor special timetables distinguish them from the rest of the citizenry. Religious tend to "value more the influence of their life attitudes and personal witness than they do the impact of service to an institution."[25] To put it another way, there is a sort of diffuse Franciscanism in our times, representing a desire to connect with the original and fundamental sense of the religious life: a life-style that is significant in itself.

3.2. *Prayer*. This same trend can be felt in the prayer life of religious. In the not-too-distant past, communities imposed numerous acts of community prayer, many of them devotional in character. Even personal meditation and spiritual reading were made into community acts. Some quite detailed methods of meditation were very popular. Apostolic communities have largely done away with these numerous community acts and have returned mental prayer to the responsibility and initiative of the individual. Initially, more than a few religious felt left in the lurch by all of this, so that one often heard the complaint, "We aren't praying anymore!" Others, on the contrary, looked upon the new approach as a license to improvise, and began to forget the lessons of the spiritual masters, lessons that were themselves the fruit of prolonged experience. We believe that this situation has been largely corrected. Left in greater liberty, religious themselves have had to face up to their responsibility. But even here, some exaggerations exist. One sometimes gets the impression that some people regard prayer as a strictly private responsibility, despite the fact that constitutions clearly represent it as an essential life-trait for all members of the institute. Our prayer life is a commitment we make to the community, and other members of the community have every right to be concerned when we give the impression that we are failing in prayer.

3.3. *A New Understanding of Law.* Another commonly observable trend is the new way in which the revised constitutions and rules of life are presented. A little background may clarify this trend. In many texts submitted to the Holy See by nineteenth century founders and foundresses, there was an overload of ascetical exhortations and a dearth of canonical structures. In reaction to this the Roman Curia, around the turn of the century, issued its *Normae secundum quas,* excluding all these ascetical passages and adding the necessary structural sections.[26] This had the unfortunate effect of reducing most constitutions to the bare bones of a canonical and disciplinary text, containing an abundance of precise norms on how to do things, on the practice of mortification, and on rules for cloister and silence. We were left with a code of precepts. In the new constitutions and rules of life, few norms remain, and those that do are canonical, almost to the exclusion of those of a purely disciplinary nature. In contrast, these new texts give us a description of the vocation and spirit of the religious who belong to each institute. We have passed, so to speak, from a "decalogue" code of observances to a "beatitudes" rule of life, from a minimum we must observe to a maximum toward which we must strive. Instead of observance, we now tend to speak of growing fidelity. St. Thomas observed long ago that the twofold Gospel precept of love (with all one's heart) is not something we fulfill here and now in an instant, but is rather a goal toward which we must constantly strive and tend. This is the evangelical vision to which the new rules of life invite us. Hence, for all their dearth of precepts, these new rules are on the whole more demanding.

3.4. *Individual and Community Discernment.* The greater freedom allotted to individuals and to local communities, the reinterpretation of the fundamental law as a description of vocation and spirit, and the relative absence of disciplinary norms have all placed a greater burden of responsibility on local communities and their members. Local communities must frequently assume the role of discerning what is here and now God's salvific will for the group and its members. In this respect, the 32nd General Congregation of the Society of Jesus has set a good example for us all. Speaking of the mission of the Jesuits today, the Congregation stated: "We must undertake a thoroughgoing assessment of our traditional apostolic methods, attitudes and institutions with a view to adapting them to the new needs of the times and to a world of rapid change. All this demands that we practice discernment, that spiritual discernment which Saint Ignatius teaches us in the Exercises. Moreover, discerning will yield a deeper grasp of the movements, aspirations and struggles in the hearts of our contemporaries."[27] A little later, the decree restates the same idea: "What is required is not so much a research program as a process of reflection and evaluation inspired by the Ignatian tradition of spiritual discernment."[28] The Ignatian practice of spiritual discernment, once largely restricted to circles of the Society of Jesus, has now become generalized to the point that it is present in all schools of spirituality. Recent bibliography abundantly bears out this development,[29] and we should all be glad of it.

Actually, the practice of group discernment, as a stage in the process of obedience, far from being something new, has its roots in a remote past. The elders of the desert used to go around to seek a word of wisdom from others who had no juridical authority on them. The infinitude of God, revealed in the complexities and richness of the religious experience, is too much for one individual. St. Benedict determines wisely in his Rule that the abbot should bring the main decisions to the whole community, in the quasi-liturgical atmosphere of the chapter, and hear what everybody has to say, since "the Lord often reveals what is better to the younger."[30]

3.5. *A Blurred Image of Church.* As we round out this section, we can hardly avoid mentioning one painful fact: the disinterest or distaste that some religious feel toward the ecclesiastical institution. Francis of Assisi, who was called to rebuild God's tottering house, was distinguished from other leaders of poverty movements in his day by his fidelity to the Church's leaders.[31] St. Ignatius Loyola, another great religious reformer, recommended that we "feel with the hierarchical Church."[32] Today, although most religious are strongly attracted to the Church as communion and mystery, a number of them tend to experience the Church institution as something alienating. The fact is that the image of the Church projected by Leo XIII, Pius XI and Pius XII has largely disappeared, and new images are struggling to emerge. There is a significant amount of writing on various "models of the Church."[33] We all know that institutions, in this earthly phase of things, are as necessary for the Church's presence and action as the body is for the self's. We must of course take care of the body and control it, since here, too, an overly heavy body can impede the action of the individual spirit.

4. MINISTERIAL OPENNESS TO THE WORD

Another group of factors that seems to constitute a characteristic trend in today's religious life is the positive reevaluation of the world and of the religious life as service to the Church and the world.[34] Isaac Hecker introduced a typically American sensibility into spirituality by underscoring the positive character of the encounter of grace with our humanity, and by consistently speaking of this encounter in positive terms.[35] The classic synthesis of Thomas Aquinas began to reappear with new accents. In the United States today, there are many spiritualities which evaluate the created world positively and associate spiritual progress with overall progress (holiness/wholeness). In Europe, Louvain accustomed us to a theology of earthly values.[36] In France, where great stress had always been laid on the incarnation, a high value was placed on Christian presence among the masses (the priest-worker movement). Vatican II, above all in *Gaudium et Spes,* gave us a realistic vision of the world that was rich in positive traits. John XXIII's *Pacem in Terris* decidedly opted for democratic social values. All of this has had its impact on the life of the Church. Secular institutes are precisely secular institutions that aim at enlivening the human and civil "world" from within. The charisms of the religious life are now spoken of, not as gifts to help us flee from the world, but rather as gifts that enable us to penetrate the world more deeply in order to transcend it. We no longer speak of a *fuga mundi,* but rather a penetration of the world, in order to induce it to return to its Creator, and transcend itself.

Thomas Merton personified this "return to the world" movement in almost paradigmatic fashion. His early works, written at a time when he regarded the Abbey of Gethsemani as "the only real city in America,"[37] reflect the critical reactions of a convert, as well as a somewhat elitist monastic theology. In *Seeds of Contemplation* (1949), the theme of a holy person's positive outlook on the world alternates with a negative view of the secular city from which the Christian must strive to escape.[38] In *The Inner Experience* (1959), his attitude toward contemplatives is more realistic, and the possibility of a lived experience of God in the world emerges more clearly.[39] One can notice an effort to situate contemplation in the living context of everyday life. Contemplation means an in-depth look at reality not in order to evade it, but in order to transcend it;[40] it supposes a reading of events.[41] The new chapter, "Solitude Is Not Separation," added to *New Seeds of Contemplation*[42] reveals at last a total contemplative openness to the world. Thomas Merton would soon become a prophet of peace and justice. The contemplative—as Teresa of Jesus had experienced long before Merton—is someone who brings the world, its agonies and its ecstasies, before God.[43]

This phenomenon has occurred frequently in the course of history. We might, in fact, speak of a phasic alternation between periods of incarnation and periods of transcendence, although we should add that each swing toward the incarnational pole has left us definitively closer to the world. The twelfth century witnessed a cultural rebirth in which "nature" began to lose its sacral, symbolic value and gained some measure of autonomy.[44] The married laity ceased being referred to as "children and weaklings who simply cannot embrace celibacy" (an oft-repeated phrase in early ecclesiastical texts),[45] and were instead spoken of as persons who profess the "common rule," that is, the Gospel. The Third Orders of the thirteenth century owe their existence, in part, to this change of mentality. In an early Franciscan legend, Madonna Poverta (Lady Poverty) asks a group of friars to show her their cloister. They lead her to the top of a hill and show her the whole world, telling her: "This, Lady, is our cloister."[46] Then came what we generally call "the Renaissance," and we fell in love with the philosophers, writers and heroes of the Greco-Roman world. A positive and overly innocent view of the world infiltrated our consciousness. Jesuits made their residence in the midst of cities. More than a few institutes of the time chose not to take vows (Oratorians and Eudists). The Daughters of Charity dispersed through the streets in peasant garb; for them the world was the space in which the sons and daughters of God were suffering. But there was also Luther's teaching on our "corrupted nature," and Bishop Jansenius and the Port Royalists held the dark view that every human value not explicitly elevated by a supernatural intention is simply sinful. Jansenism, with its excessive moral demands, had a baneful influence on the spirituality of religious. Finally, the trauma of the French and socialist revolutions filled religious leaders with fears and misapprehensions, so that they tended to stress the deep incompatibility between the Church and modern society. We were in urgent need of a return to the world.

4.1. *A More Positive Vision of the World.* For religious, too, the world is the *ager dominicus,* the Lord's field. It is the creation wounded by our sins, yet fundamentally good; the place where we must live our faith, hope and love, and in which we must work and suffer. This more positive, yet realistic vision of the world has positive consequences and gives rise to its own problematic. The distance between the religious and secular worlds has been shortened. The barriers of habits, special buildings and institutions filled with religious symbols, have largely fallen. This explains a number of recent developments. In the past, new forms of religious life inexorably fell under the influence of forms that had a longer and more prestigious history: Pachomians and Basilians became monks; canons regular and mendicants adopted a monastic or quasi-monastc way of life; apostolic congregations of women imitated cloistered nuns, etc. In our times, the trend seems to be running in the opposite direction: the traditional forms of religious life are getting closer to the life-style of secular institutes. We are referring here not merely to the absence of habits or the irrelevance of details that were once considered very important in Europe (such as not being allowed to enter a movie theater), but to such truly important items as the near absence of community life or its reduction to a minimum, and to the growing trend toward working in secular institutions.

The fact remains, however, that religious life, precisely because its witness is aimed at helping the world transcend itself, must not only incarnate itself in secular culture, but also act as a counterculture.[47] Religious life accomplishes this essentially by actualizing the charisms that distinguish it as a form of Christian life: celibacy and community, with a public witness of poverty. Note that we say celibacy, not bachelorhood or the single state, since celibacy is understood as an exclusive commitment to the concerns of the Lord, and as a life lived for the love of the Lord. And this is extremely demanding. So also is the radical self-divestment which characterizes the Christian poverty of a religious: a self-divestment that makes no sense at all except as an act of solidarity with the poor and the outcast. All of this must be reflected in our life-style, attitudes and options.

The new Code of Canon Law (607.3) uses the old monastic concept of "separation from the world" to refer to this public attitude toward the human secular society, and this is proper to religious life. We should notice carefully that the canon intends to describe a few "essential elements" of religious life, which are found in different ways in institutions as different among themselves as the Trappists, the Carmel, the Institute of the Blessed Virgin Mary, the Society of Jesus, the Paulists, and the Little Sisters of the Poor. This is why the canon does not speak of the separation from the world in absolute terms, but of that separation which is proper to the nature and purpose of each institution. Originally this "separation" was expressed through a material distance, and later through the enclosure. Then some canons regular and the mendicants created a movement of osmosis and exosmosis with the laity. Finally communities were created to evangelize or to assist the needy outside. The image and the experience of the human world differs profoundly in each case.

And yet a movement of transcending the secular society is visible in all. We believe that this movement is radically expressed through our commitment to become celibate for the reign of God and through our profession of Christian poverty. In some religious, this movement is further expressed through solitude (hermits, contemplative institutions); in others by creating in the midst of human society a parabolic form of Christian community: sisters or brothers face together the city in order to assist those whom society rejects and the rest of the Church tends sometimes to forget. Let us suffice to remember the peasants left by the clergy in their ignorance, and the poor dying unassisted, in the times of John of God, Vincent de Paul, and Louise de Marillac.

4.2. *An Open Community.* Our communities have opened up. The practice of hospitality has been greatly enlarged. Religious are praying and working with groups outside the community proper, thus creating a network of relationships. Many of us belong to prayer groups (charismatic or otherwise) or to pastoral teams.[48] Monastery guesthouses, especially in the United States, are usually filled with other religious and lay persons who come there to pray. Some contemplative monasteries have opened up to share their prayer life with others on a more permanent basis. The Trappists of Our Lady of Guadalupe have established a Center for Contemplative Studies. The Carmel of the Resurrection in Indianapolis has opened its prayer life to a group of the faithful who pray there. Many small apostolic communities practice an apostolate of presence by living among the poor. This is something that the mendicants strove to do in the thirteenth century, and which the Little Brothers and Sisters of Jesus reintroduced some decades ago. Obviously, such groups have to manage the difficult task of balancing their openness toward the rest of the Church with the special communion of charism and spirit they must keep among their own members.

4.3. *Celibacy and Friendship.* One effect of this optimistic vision of the world and of the human person in the world has been the rediscovery of the positive and fully human vision of celibacy expressed in the New Testament. Although Jesus, in his *logion* about eunuchs (Mt 19:12), was defending a spiritual impotence caused by a strong commitment to the kingdom, Paul tells us, in a positive way, that being celibate for the sake of the Gospel consists in living lives exclusively dedicated to the concerns of the risen Lord (his Church, his poor), and his love (1 Cor 7:32–34). Celibacy is both a commitment and relationship of love in which we can grow, and not simply a state defined by non-bonding to another person in matrimony.[49] The focus of today's religious has shifted, significantly, from chastity to celibacy as a way of life. From yet another point of view, the modern notion of the human being has highlighted (sometimes excessively) our sexual condition. Sexuality is rightly understood as a positive reality,[50] in which affective balance plays an important part. Thus conceived, sexuality is being incorporated into a positive and inclusive vision of celibacy. It might be noted, in passing, that religious, like others in this rich culture which is concerned with overeating, also engage in sports and look after their body and physical appearance.

But it must be admitted that the fall of barriers in this context (locked doors, permission to go out, opened mail, the habit, etc.) also eliminated a series of social pressures aimed at protecting celibacy. Just as the permanence of marriage is now left to married couples themselves (since urban and industrialized society, unlike rural societies of the past, undermines rather than upholds the stability of marriage), so celibacy is left to the grace of God and the responsibility of the individual. The community can offer little help to those in crisis, except prayer and friendship. A positive evaluation of friendship has important consequences in this area. The husband-wife relationship is beginning to pale as the only model for male-female relationships. Friendships between religious and persons of the opposite sex (whether priests, religious or laity) are now more feasible and frequent.[51] This is, of course, not something completely new: a good number of saints, especially founders and foundresses, seem to have come in pairs. But now there is a greater awareness of the implications and values of friendship as a help toward celibate balance, which it indeed can be. But this is still fragile ground, because of the possibility of being "carried away," and because the word "friendship" often covers a number of relationships of diverse intensity.[52] The celibate is committed to live exclusively for the concerns of the Lord and for his love, and this rules out not just physical relationships, but also exclusive affective commitments. This means that certain affective needs of the celibate cannot be satisfied directly, but must be diverted into channels of loving service.

4.4. *The Poor: the New "Desert."*[53] Religious feel a lively interest and concern for the world of which they are part. This is quite apparent in questions of justice. In a host of ways, religious have been associated with works of charity throughout history. But today there is a clearer consciousness that not a few evils have social roots, and that religious in a democratic society have a great opportunity to work collectively and individually in defense of the weak and the oppressed. Most of us (even religious dedicated to social works) inherited a vision of poverty that did not have much of an express or lived relationship to the poor of the world. It was a poverty fit for a neo-platonic or neo-pythagorean community: a poverty understood as a form of personal purification and as a means for arriving more readily at contemplation. The important thing was dependence on the superior, and great individual austerity. On an analogy with the Synoptic saying of Jesus, "Sell what you have and give to the poor" (Mk 10:21 and par.), one might say that the monks of the desert, who worked hard to support the poor, fulfilled the second part of the saying ("and give to the poor"), whereas later religious stressed the first part ("sell what you have"). In *Evangelica Testificatio,* Paul VI brought the Church's teaching on religious poverty back to its origins by beginning the section on poverty with a call to hear "the cry of the poor."[54] If all Christian poverty is a descent with Christ into the hell of human suffering—a participation in his *kenosis* (cf. 2 Cor 8:9)[55]—then the testimonial poverty of religious should signal an abandonment of the world's logic and a crossing over its borders into the new desert which, especially in today's materialistic society, is constituted by the poor.

A number of religious have abandoned their houses in middle-class neighborhoods and have gone to live with the poor in ghettos. Whole institutes have declared in their chapters a preferential option for evangelizing the poor. Religious men and women have joined other Christians in their struggle for the liberation of the poor, especially in Latin America and the Philippines. In the United States, some religious have run for national or state office in defense of minorities, while others have been appointed to posts of particular social significance. Many U.S. religious are committed to a variety of social causes: disarmament, human rights in the third world, the rights of the unborn, the rights of homosexuals, ecology, the struggle against a capitalism that would sacrifice human lives for economic gain (the Nestlé boycott), and so forth.

Here again, there are problems and difficulties. For one thing, it is easier for those living in well-to-do environments to protest abuses (as they must) than it is to protect themselves against the contagion of a consumerist society. Those who are truly and deeply committed to the defense of the poor know that they can carry out their work only by becoming poor themselves. Our poverty is also a protest against a materialistic interpretation of life, and hence must be manifested in personal and collective simplicity and austerity. Those who personally commit themselves to poverty run the risk of mere improvisation, or of being manipulated by others. One thinks of the way certain reactionary thinkers have tried to use Mother Teresa of Calcutta, proposing her as an example of what all religious should be doing—which they interpret as gathering up the dying from the sidewalks (which is undoubtedly a heroically beautiful act of Christian love), and then leaving the world to the powers that be (which would undoubtedly be an act of un-Christian cowardice, since the one behind the "powers that be" is often Satan, the first murderer).

Manipulation, though, is also practiced from a revolutionary viewpoint. There is a danger of becoming involved in partisan politics that pursue a determined type of society. The religious and the Christian as such do not have a distinctive political model, but only a set of fundamental principles (*Pacem in Terris*), according to which they raise their voice in protest against all forms that oppress and manipulate the sons and daughters of God. Great maturity is required for a commitment of this kind. One must be prepared to lose one's life: witness the example of our martyrs in Central America.

4.5. *Serving in a Secular Milieu*. With growing frequency, religious men and women are making a commitment in various types of human service that are not specifically religious in nature, and are performed in a secular environment. We are referring here mainly to those religious who are engaged in the investigation and teaching of profane disciplines. Religious have been doing this for centuries, of course, but as an integral part of a ministry of Christian education that was meant to culminate in catechesis. Now we encounter a new element in that these services are being carried on in the heart of secular centers. The impact of this environment and the great demand for professional preparation it calls for can profoundly affect the spirit of a religious. This is perhaps most true of religious who practice psychotherapy in its various forms. Here the "secular environment" is internal. The religious has to operate with a series of symbols, vocabularies and techniques in which religious experience is often treated either in the context of psychological aberration, or else (as with Jung) in that of a psychic activity that neither includes nor excludes grace. Helping one's neighbors in their psychological problems, or contributing to their overall growth as persons, is just as religious an activity as helping cure their bodies, but it can create difficulties for religious therapists. Oftentimes they are living in an environment quite different from a traditional religious community, which was pervaded by religious symbols and community acts. In such cases, religious will often have to struggle in order to integrate their professional service into the framework of their community's proper spirituality. Service also tends to change meaning for religious who work as medical or nursing personnel in modern hospitals, with their intense activity and the difficulties they present for establishing personal relationships with the sick, since there are so many to attend, and the turnover is so rapid.

Paul VI in his *Evangelica Testificatio* has addressed a few words of encouragement and exhortation to these religious: "Many of you will be obliged to lead your lives, at least in part, in a world which tends to exile human beings from themselves and to compromise both their spiritual unity and their union with God. You must therefore learn to find God even under those conditions of life which are marked by an increasingly accelerated rhythm and by the noise and the attraction of the ephemeral."[56]

5. RELIGIOUS LIFE REINTERPRETED

5.1. A More Profound Notion of the Religious Life. The Second Vatican Council, by setting its teaching on the religious life squarely in the context of the life of the Church and of the universal call to holiness, forced theologians to rethink this particular vocation. A significant index of this rethinking is reflected in a change in the bibliography on the religious life. During the first half of this century, it focused on Canon Law and ascetical conferences or retreats for religious; from the Council onward, bibliographical entries of a theological character began to multiply. New Testament exegesis began to put question marks after the texts on which some founders had based their movements. Often enough, disturbingly, exegetes answered these questions in the negative: "This is not what these biblical texts were saying." Moreover, the full incorporation of the secular laity into the life and holiness of the Church obliged us to rethink the relationship that exists between the call to the religious life and the general call to perfection, as well as that which exists between religious life and secular life.

In more than one case, the Council had felt obliged to use categories drawn from Scholasticism, in a clear effort at expanding its teaching. Concomitantly, however, scholars were at work compiling critical studies of the sources of the religious life (Pachomius, Basil, Augustine, the anonymous author of the *Regula Magistri,* Benedict, Francis, early Jesuit texts, etc.). These historical investigations have given us a much better knowledge of the development of the religious life. The works of Tillard, Boff, Sebastian, Maloney and others, as well as the publications of the Religious Life Institutes in Rome and Madrid, and those of the Claret Center for Resources in Spirituality (to all three of which I have made my personal contribution), are developing a work of synthesis that has become necessary.

5.2. Religious Life: A Parable of Discipleship. In *Lumen Gentium* and *Perfectae Caritatis,* the Second Vatican Council abandoned the notion of "state of perfection," which had somehow crept into *Sacrosanctum Concilium* (the Constitution on the Liturgy), written in the period before the Council began to reflect expressly on the religious life.[57] All Christians are committed to growth in the perfection to which they are called in baptism, confirmation, the Eucharist and reconciliation, and (for some) eventually in matrimony. The religious life is no longer to be thought of as the only state in which one professes to be tending toward perfection. In *Discipleship: Towards an Understanding of the Religious Life,* I tried to demonstrate how religious life is a form of discipleship, and that the significance of the religious life consists in its being a living parable of the Gospel for all. As a form of life, the religious life is summoned to remind all Christ's disciples of the demand to follow him. It is a type of prophetic life, neither more nor less. This leaves room for secular Christians to achieve the full stature of their incorporation into evangelical spirituality. For the important thing is not the parable, but the lived life of the Christian way, to which the parable points.

5.3. *Return to Charism*. Another important aspect of contemporary religious life is the fact that, thanks mainly to the invitation of *Perfectae Caritatis*, religious institutes, especially in their chapters of renewal, have set about reflecting on their own charisms. These institutes now seem to have a far better knowledge of their vocation and spirit in the Church. The Church itself is enriched by this variety of charisms. The Popes have frequently referred to this theme in discussing the identity of religious families.

5.4. *Turning Toward Others*. Nevertheless, something new is happening. A few years back, religious institutes often gave the impression of being overly exclusive in promoting their own interests. There was too much insistence on "our own." Today, religious communities collaborate with one another in common novitiate programs. There are theologates (the Central Theological Union in Chicago and General Theological Union in Berkeley are obvious examples) in which students from various institutes study, pray together and interrelate in many ways, thus mutually enriching one another without losing their identity. And there are numerous religious institutes collaborating in apostolic works, both with one another and with lay team members. The sense of belonging to the one Church of Christ is thus manifested in a forceful manner.

6. LIFELONG COMMITMENT

One aspect which involves considerable suffering for many religious and which is brought up with some frequency in public meetings and private conversations, is the meaningfulness of a perpetual commitment to the religious life, and even the legitimacy of norms that impose this sort of commitment toward the end of one's initiation or formation. Obviously, the discussion of this theme is less related to the influence of any specific philosophy than it is to the fact that our society seems to be much more sensitive to change than to continuity. In our society, for several different reasons, it is not rare for persons to change careers at a certain age. Even marriage seems to be becoming more fragile.[58]

6.1. *A Personal Commitment.* In contradistinction to a one-time or short-term commitment to do some *thing,* a commitment to a type of *life* is a personal project that requires a certain amount of time to make. Human beings develop gradually. A promise or decision to be celibate or to live for the love of someone else for just a few days or weeks would really be tantamount to a commitment to do some *thing* rather than a *life decision* to be a determined type of man or woman. The commitment to love is, of its very nature, indefinite as to time. It tends to be projected over a whole lifetime. The fact is that, when a human being loves or chooses to give himself or herself on a deep level, he or she cannot include the idea of a temporal limit in such a choice (although there may be an implicit recognition of the possibility of failure), since this would be restricting one's love or self-gift. By making a commitment of oneself, a person aims at putting his or her love above time and its changes.

6.2. *A Commitment to God.* A commitment to the religious life entails a commitment to build one's life with an orientation toward certain religious ideals: living in a particular way, in celibacy and in community. Here, the depth of human commitment is at its greatest, since it is gauged by a relationship with God. In this case, understandably, our intention must exclude every temporal limit, even when we are making a temporal commitment. We want to be this type of Christian and human being on the deepest level, before God and in the Church. This is a quite different kind of commitment than that made by a person who would simply like to be associated with the life, spirituality and ministry of a religious community for a set period of time. One thinks, for example, of the existing practice in Thailand whereby all boys, as a sort of analogue of military service, must spend several months in a Buddhist monastery. This sort of procedure might well be adopted, in a more systematic way, for certain types of associates of Christian religious communities. But this kind of temporal commitment, even when made on a more conscious and voluntary basis, would never suffice to constitute the person making it a religious. Our temporal vows are truly vows, to the extent that the person making them has the intention of orienting his or her whole life in this manner.

6.3. *A Statement of Commitment.* The real problem here refers to the public formulation of this intention to make a perpetual commitment. To express ourselves publicly and socially is an essential trait of our human nature, which never exists in a vacuum of pure interiority, but tends to unfold itself in explicit relationship with others. We already made our perpetual commitment when we responded to our vocation, before entering a community. We made it with a certain tension, with some misgivings, and sometimes even with anguish; yet we entrusted our weakness to the grace of the God who called us. On professing, we renewed this response to God, but this time we did so publicly, before God, and through the community we committed ourselves to God through this community. Our commitment, then, took on an ecclesial character. This was normal and as it should be because promising to be celibate, to live in evangelical poverty and in community is not just an act that relates us directly to God. Rather, it is an act that relates us to God in his Church. Celibacy is not just the love of God, but also a great love of his sons and daughters.

This does not rule out our foreseeing possible failures, or even the hypothetical possibility that certain experiences and circumstances might make us change. This commitment is made by human persons, with the understanding that they are expressing their actual intention, in the hope that this intention will perdure. But since fidelity in this matter is the work of grace, we place all our forces in

God's hands. A religious vow or promise is at once a manifestation of our intention and a petition for grace: "This is what I intend to be, so help me God."

The person who makes a vow can change, can fail, or can discover that this was not to be his or her permanent vocation. There are canonized saints who, after years of profession, left their communities when they discovered that God was calling them along another way. For all these reasons, the Church wisely grants dispensations from these commitments. A dispensation dissolves the canonical aspects of one's commitment, leaving the person with his or her responsibility before God intact. Upon receiving their dispensations, these Christians remain in God's presence, just as they did at the time they believed they had received a call from God and answered it.

7. A PROPHETIC MINORITY?

The aerial photograph we promised at the beginning of this survey is not yet complete. We still need to include in it one of the most visibly preoccupying concerns for many religious and for the Church's ministers: the scarcity of vocations to the religious life which we are presently experiencing. There is no need for us to go into statistical details. All we have to do is to look at the inexorably upward trend in the median age of the members of most religious communities in the northern hemisphere. We can only suppose that what we are looking at is precisely a lack of vocations (God is calling fewer men and women to the religious life), and not a lack of correspondence to a wider call. We must suppose this, both because we do not have access to the heavenly archives, and because we find it hard to believe that human beings are currently putting up a greater resistance to grace than they did in the days when our houses were filled to the rafters. One fact confirms us in our rejection of an unduly pessimistic view of the present generation: the growing number of vocations to the ministry outside the clergy and outside religious institutes.

People continue to cite a whole litany of causes in order to explain the current dearth of candidates for the religious life: economic reasons (greater opportunities exist elsewhere today); social reasons (secularized environment, lowered prestige of the religious state, easier relations among young people of both sexes, sexual liberation, smaller families of the "one girl-one boy" type); psychological reasons (the identity crisis of religious makes religious life less attractive; pessimism or a lost sense of belonging leads religious to work less at promoting vocations); theological reasons (religious life is not the only state for attaining Christian perfection). We would not like to indulge in a discussion of the many reasons alleged to explain this phenomenon.

We would, however, like to point out that we are not talking about a scarcity of persons who want to enter a religious community, but about the considerably smaller number of persons who show clear signs of having a true vocation to the religious life. All you have to do is run a few ads in the right publications, and you will soon be swarming with requests. Some of these aspirants very soon reveal data that indicate their unfitness for the religious life. A few more serious cases must be rejected somewhat later, either after psychological testing or after a few days of shared life. Present-day religious life requires stronger and more balanced personalities than was the case in the past. Formerly, less well-balanced personalities could be kept in line by a tougher practice of authority and by the more disciplinary type of community that then prevailed.

Permit me to make a few observations. Until two or three decades ago, becoming a priest or a religious was the only route that enabled a Christian to consecrate his or her life to ministry in the Church. Of course, there were many Christians who were dedicated to charitable works and catechesis on a part-time basis. But if they wanted to orient their whole life to one of these ministries, they had no recourse but to become priests or religious. The need was even greater in the case of women, since they did not have a choice between secular priesthood and the religious life. Any woman who wanted to commit her life to a ministry of charity or catechesis had to become a religious. The call to one was automatically interpreted as a call to the other. But today it is possible, though at times difficult, for a Christian to be committed to a ministry without becoming a priest or a religious.

In the past, every time a new form of religious life, better adapted to the conditions of the time, appeared, there tended to be a diminution of candidates for the forms that had prevailed up to that time. Before the twelfth century, Europe had numerous monasteries; next, it witnessed the rise of whole armies of mendicants; at length, the mendicants had to share the scene with clerks regular. Also in Europe, until about the middle of the last century, there were cloistered convents in most middle-sized towns. But with the foundation of numerous apostolic congregations for women, the number of cloistered convents diminished considerably. Today, secular institutes and other associations of Christian life have appeared on the scene. Moreover, the Church has begun to open up its ministries to laypersons who have no connection with any institution. This must necessarily lead to a reduction in the number of candidates for the religious life.

Hence, we should not be talking about a lack of vocations in an unqualified way, because the Spirit of the Lord is continuing to call Christians of all sorts to a whole gamut of commitments. We should joyfully accept the Spirit's will. It is quite possible—given our inveterate resistance in this respect—that the only way the secular laity will be able to take their rightful place in the Church's ministry will be through a considerable reduction in the number of priests and religious. Hard as some of us may find it to accept these persons on equal terms, despite their manifest charisms and responsibilities, the Spirit of the Lord may oblige us to accept them out of necessity.

Does this mean that religious life in its traditional forms is destined in the future, even more than in the present and the past, to become a minority life-style? That is certainly a possibility, although we would not like to hazard such a prediction. Because history has passed through so many ups and downs, turns and returns, visions and revisions, it ill becomes a historian, who has had a hard enough task sorting out the vagaries of the past, to presume to know the future. But if things did happen to turn out in the way we have hypothesized, there would be nothing to be surprised at. After all, we have described the religious life as a prophetic calling. And isn't a truly prophetic mission always and essentially a minority calling?

NOTES

1. Thomas Dubay offers one answer in *What Is Religious Life? Questions Religious Are Asking* (Denville, N.J.: Dimension Books, 1979), pp. 32–34. See C. Maloney, "Evangelization and Social Change," *Religious and the Evangelization of the World, Donum Dei* Series, no. 21 (Ottawa: Publications of the Canadian Religious Conference, 1974), p. 63. See also B. Boyce, C.SS.R., "A Sociological Appraisal of the New Trends," *New Trends in Religious Life, Donum Dei* Series, no. 14 (1969), p. 135.

2. Thaddée Matura, O.F.M., *The Crisis of Religious Life* (Chicago: Franciscan Herald Press, 1974).

3. Karl Rahner, S.J., "Toward a Fundamental Theological Interpretation of Vatican II," *Theological Studies 40* (1979), p. 717.

4. John XXIII, *Mater et Magistra,* AAS 53 (1961), p. 417. *Gaudium et Spes,* no. 74, *Vatican Council II: The Conciliar and Post Conciliar Documents,* ed. Austin Flannery (Collegeville: Liturgical Press, 1975), p. 981.

5. *Constitutions* S.J., ch. IV, 10 no. 5; *Claretian Constitutions* (1865), I, no. 31.

6. Viatorians (1979), no. 52; de La Salle (1976), no. 140, 1; Precious Blood Sisters, O'Fallon, P. 54; Combonians (1979), no. 103; Christian Brothers (E. Rice), no. 247.

7. Sisters of Charity of the Incarnate Word, no. 26; Marianists, *Rule of Life* (1981), no. 39; Stigmatines (1977), no. 17. See especially Sisters of Mercy, Covenant, Fellowship and Total Growth, pp. F 4–5; Combonians, no. 42.

8. This idea forms the background for the sections on the vows in many revised constitutions.

9. St. Thomas Aquinas, *Summa Theologiae,* 2-2, q. 184 a. 2; St. Bonaventure, *Apologia Pauperum,* ch. 3, no. 3. See *Lumen Gentium,* no. 44, Flannery, pp. 403–404.

10. The theme of various personal gifts appears frequently in the new constitutions. See Sisters of St. Joseph, *Core Constitutions,* no. 38; Combonians, *Rule of Life,* nos. 38.1, 42; de La Salle (1976), p. 36; B.V.M., no. 3; Marists (1968), no. 51; Stigmatines (1977), no. 17; St. Joseph of Peace (1968), p. 6; Ursulines of Belleville (1982), no. 33; Sinsinawa Dominicans, no. 10.

11. Cited in Paulist *Provisional Constitutions* (1970), no. 9.

12. Society of the Precious Blood, no. 39; Sisters of Mercy, *Core Constitutions,* p. 27; *31st Congregation of the Society of Jesus,* Decree 17, no. 7 (St. Louis: Institute of Jesuit Sources, 1977), p. 161.

13. Quentin Hakenewerth, S.M., "Illustrations of Fundamental Choices and Their Consequences," *Religious Life Tomorrow, Donum Dei* Series, no. 24 (1978), p. 187.

14. Claretians, no. 102 ff.; Piarists, no. 131 ff.; Combonians, no. 105 ff.; School Sisters of Notre Dame, II, no. 8 ff.; Sisters of St. Joseph of Carondelet, no. 25 ff.; Society of the Sacred Heart of Jesus, no. 138 ff.

15. Scalabrinians, no. 10; Society of Mary, no. 34 ff.; Society of the Precious Blood, no. 6 ff.

16. No. 40, Flannery, pp. 698–699.

17. No. 14, Flannery, pp. 619–620.

18. The vocabulary of the revised constitutions on this theme, and the very horizons on which they move, reveal a new sensibility. When one com-

pares them to the relevant sections in *Perfectae Caritatis,* one sees that the latter opened but a single door. A smaller number of constitutions chose to remain within the limits in which the conciliar decree moves.

19. See Jesuits, *31st General Congregation,* Decree 17, pp. 157–166.

20. *Perfectae Caritatis,* no. 3, Flannery, p. 613.

21. J. Doyle, B.V.M., "Choose Life," *Religious Life Tomorrow, Donum Dei* Series, no. 24 (1978), pp. 28–31.

22. See M. Linscott, "The Religious Woman in the Church," *Way Supplement* 19 (1973), pp. 45–62.

23. No. 44, Flannery, pp. 402–403.

24. *Ibid.,* pp. 403–405.

25. Hakenewerth, *art. cit.,* p. 186.

26. "Normae secundum quas S. Congregatio Episcoporum et Regularium procedere solet in approbandis novis Institutis votorum simplicium." Published by Ladislaus Ravasi, C.P. in *De Regulis et Constitutionibus Religiosorum* (Roma: Desclee, 1958), pp. 188 ff. To be excluded from the constitutions: quotations from the Holy Scriptures, Councils and Fathers . . . (n. 27), ascetic instructions, spiritual exhortations, mystical considerations (no. 33).

27. *Documents of the 31st and 32nd General Congregations of the Society of Jesus* (St. Louis: Institute of Jesuit Sources, 1979) Decree 4, nos. 58–59, p. 413.

28. *Ibid.,* no. 74, 436.

29. Scanning the bibliography on discernment during the last fifteen years (published by the Religious Formation Conference), I have counted eleven articles in *Review for Religious,* 11 in *Way Supplement,* three in *Sisters Today,* and two each in *The Way* and *Spiritual Life.*

30. RB 3.3.

31. St. Francis of Assisi, Rule 1221, Foreword and ch. 19; Rule 1223, ch. 1; ch. 9; Testament, See *Writings and Early Biographies* (Chicago: Franciscan Herald Press, 1973), pp. 31, 46, 57, 63, 67.

32. St. Ignatius of Loyola, "To have the true sentiment which we ought to have in the Church Militant," 1st Rule. See David A. Fleming, *The Spiritual Exercises* (St. Louis: The Institute of Jesuit Sources, 1978), p. 230.

33. See Avery Dulles, S.J., *Models of the Church* (Garden City: Doubleday, 1974).

34. Cardinal Suenen's *The Nun in the World* (Westminster: The Newman Press, 1963), an invitation to the renewal of women's religious life issued during the Council, started with a chapter on the world, followed by a chapter on women and their emancipation. The book was highly successful in its time.

35. See Martin Kirk, C.M.F., "The Spirituality of Isaac Thomas Hecker: Reconciling the American Character and the Catholic Faith" (doctoral dissertation, St. Louis University, 1980).

36. See Gustave Thils, *Theologie des Réalités Terrestres* (Bruges: Desclée de Brouwer, 1946). An epoch-making book. By the same author: *Christian Attitudes* (Chicago: Scepper, 1959), 96 pp.

37. *The Secular Journal*, April 7, 1941 (New York: Noonday, 1977), p. 183.

38. *Seeds of Contemplation* (Norfolk: New Directions, 1949), pp. 20–23; 60–61.

39. Texts from the Inner Experience published by William H. Shannon, *Thomas Merton's Dark Path, The Inner Experience of a Contemplative* (New York: Farrar-Straus-Giroux, 1981), pp. 136–141.

40. *Ibid.*, p. 131.

41. *Ibid.*, p. 124.

42. *New Seeds of Contemplation* (New York: New Directions, 1974), pp. 52–63.

43. St. Teresa of Jesus, *Way of Perfection*, 1,2; 3,1; *Mansions*, Epilogue, 4.

44. M.-D. Chenu, O.P., *Nature, Man and Society in the Twelfth Century* (University of Chicago Press, 1968).

45. See John M. Lozano, C.M.F., *Discipleship: Towards an Understanding of the Religious Life* (Chicago: Claret Center for Resources in Spirituality, 1980), pp. 49–53.

46. *Sacrum Commercium*, no. 63, *St. Francis of Assisi: Omnibus of Sources* (Chicago: Franciscan Herald Press, 1973), p. 1593.

47. John F. Kavanaugh, S.J. has given particular attention to this theme in his *Following Christ in a Consumer Society* (Maryknoll: Orbis Books, 1981), pp. 131–142.

48. The *Constitutions of the Sisters of Charity of the Blessed Virgin Mary*, in the first chapter, contain this significant text on the new attitude: "Since we participate simultaneously in various communities—the world community, the Christian community, the entire B.V.M. community and the local community—it is the responsibility and privilege of each sister to contribute to each of these communities according to her gifts and circumstances" (no. 3).

49. See Lozano, *op. cit.*, pp. 142–170.

50. Marc Oraison, *The Celibate Condition and Sex* (New York: Sheed and Ward, 1967). See D. Goergen, *The Sexual Celibate* (New York: Seabury, 1975); K. Clarke, O.F.M., Cap., *An Experience of Celibacy* (Notre Dame: Ave Maria, 1982).

51. Also significant is the number of articles published lately on friendship between religious and persons of the opposite sex they are oriented to. In *Sisters Today*, N. Neuman, O.S.B., has published two articles (October 1974 and November 1976), and J. Becker has published one (May 1979). In *Review for Religious*, I counted four: C. Kiesling (July 1971), T. Dubay (November 1977), B. O'Leary (March 1980) and V. Peter (March–April 1982). There is another by Y. E. Raguin in *Way Supplement 19*.

52. Some constitutions and complementary statutes now speak positively of the relationship between friendship in general and celibacy: Marianists, *Rule of Life*, II, no. 2.4; Piarists, no. 57; Sisters of Charity of the B.V.M., no. 33; Sinsinawa Dominicans, no. 13; Sisters of Saint Joseph of LaGrange, *Working Document* (1979), no. 42. Some texts treat of the relationship between celibacy and friendship with Christ: Jesuits, *31st General Congregation*, Decree 15, no. 8, p. 152; Combonians, no. 26.1. Or they speak of friendship as the fruit of celibacy: Jesuits, *op. cit.*, pp. 152–153; Brothers of the Christian Schools, 5d. Or they view friendship as a defense of celibacy: Jesuits, *ibid.* Other texts restrict their remarks to friendship within the community: Stigmatines (1982), no. 15; Holy Cross (men), no. 65; Scalabrinians, no. 80.

53. See A. Cussianovich, S.D.B., *Religious Life and the Poor* (Maryknoll: Orbis Books, 1979).

54. *Evangelica Testificatio*, no. 17, Flannery, p. 688; *Sacrosanctum Concilium*, nos. 98, 101.

55. See Lozano, *op. cit.*, "Poverty and the Kenosis of Christ," pp. 191–192.

56. *Evangelica Testificatio*, no. 33, Flannery, p. 696.

57. *Sacrosanctum Concilium*, no. 98, 101 (December 4, 1963), A. Flannery (pp. 27–28) translates "religious."

58. On this theme, see T. Matura, O.F.M., *op. cit.*, pp. 72–78.

RELIGIOUS LEADERSHIP IN A TIME OF CULTURAL CHANGE

Thomas E. Clarke, S.J.

> Thomas E. Clarke, S.J. has provided extraordinary conceptual leadership to both men and women religious in the United States during recent years. A life-long professor of theology, Clarke has increasingly served as a theological consultant to religious communities and source of stimulating reflection on the evolution of religious life.
> The following essay is a distillation of Clarke's reflections on the role of religious leadership at the present time. It was written specifically for this volume, and includes a commentary on other essays in the volume.

My privileged contribution to this volume aims to set the CMSM experience described in the preceding essays within a specific interpretive framework. This reflection on the CMSM journey itself represents a journey. About three years ago, as part of an LCWR seminar, I adapted the work done by Gibson Winter and especially by Joe Holland on "root metaphors" for a delineation of three culturally based approaches to religious life.[1] In the present essay I wish to use the same three paradigms in commenting on the CMSM story of the past few decades.[2]

The LCWR Seminar in 1982 took place prior to two relevant actions of the hierarchical Church: first, the promulgation of the new

---

1. See *LCWR Seminar Papers: Religious Congregations Within the Church*, LCWR, 1982; G. Winter, *Liberating Creation: Foundations of Religious Social Ethics,* New York: Crossroad, 1981; J. Holland, "Linking Social Analysis and Theological Reflection: The Place of Root Metaphor in Social and Religious Experience," J. Hug (ed.), *Tracing the Spirit: Communities, Social Action, and Theological Reflection,* New York: Paulist 1983, pp. 170–191.

2. This essay is not canonical (though I will be commenting on Canon Law) but theological, and different in the genre of its theology both from the "dogmatic" (or "magisterial") theology exercised more or less immediately in the adjuncts of hierarchical office, and from academic theology of the kind practiced on university campuses and in scholarly journals. It is an effort at theological reflection; I understand this term to refer to a reflective appropriation of Christian experience carried out in the environs of some basic Christian community, and aimed at the ongoing transformation of the experience or praxis of that community. In passing let me say that I consider theological reflection in this sense to be congruous with the artistic metaphor, just as dogmatic and academic theologies are, respectively, congruous with the organic and mechanistic metaphors. See my essay, "A New Way: Reflecting on Experience," in J. Hug, *op. cit.,* pp. 13–37.

law of the Church in January 1983, and, second, the letter of John Paul II to the U.S. bishops in April 1983 calling them to a special pastoral service to U.S. religious. This letter was accompanied by a document on the essentials of religious life issued for apostolic religious throughout the Church by the Sacred Congregation for Religious and for Secular Institutes (SCRIS). These new resources provide fresh illustrations, especially of the first and second paradigms, and reflection on them has deepened my conviction of the value of the root metaphor approach to cultural analysis of the life of the Church, including religious life.

In what follows I will first sketch out the "root metaphor" paradigm. Then I will indicate how this paradigm can be employed for characterizing different approaches to theologizing about religious life and to shaping its structures. Finally I will offer some observations on the preceding essays, and conclude with several brief remarks on the implications of all this for leadership in the years ahead.

I

Only a brief summary of the Winter/Holland paradigm is possible here. I would say, first, that the term "metaphor" points to a level or way of knowing that is more iconic or imaged than conceptual. It also suggests that beneath various analytical models and paradigms lie more amorphous gatherings of psycho-spiritual energy which obscurely permeate and enliven the workings of the rational/pragmatic intellect. The term "*root* metaphor" hints that some such gatherings are so primordial and comprehensive in carrying a common cultural experience that they constitute the hidden horizon or *Denkform* which permeates specific concepts and terms expressive of that experience. Thus, for example, the term "authority" is capable, with whatever difficulty, of being defined in broad or strict senses, and from the perspectives of various disciplines. But where the term is being used on the basis of one root metaphor rather than another, it mediates a meaning which can be fully grasped only in relationship to that metaphor.

From such a standpoint Joe Holland speaks of three historical stages of the Church's response to industrialization. More broadly, the response was to modernization, secularization, the Enlightenment. The first response was a negative reaction based on a cultural attachment to the pre-modern *organic* metaphor which permeated the medieval Church; it was a refusal to accommodate to the industrial revolution, the Enlightenment, modernity. The second response was precisely such an accommodation, and it entailed the acceptance of the *mechanistic* metaphor which had displaced the organic metaphor in the shaping of history. The third response, still in the early stages of its influence, is based on an *artistic* metaphor, which has the power, Winter and Holland believe, to provide a creative resolution of the impasse situation resulting from the clash of the first two metaphors.

Though this identification of the root metaphor paradigm is a mere skeleton, I hope to provide flesh for it in what follows. Building on the plausible ecclesiological correlations of Joe Holland, I would argue that today we are dealing with three distinctive, competing but also overlapping conceptions of religious life, corresponding more or less to the mindsets encouraged by each of the three root metaphors. I will call the first conception feudal/Tridentine, the second liberal/ Enlightenment, and the third radical/post-Enlightenment. Each of these conceptions entails a peculiar historical, philosophical, theological, and cultural orientation and consciousness.

II

1. Religious Life in the Organic Metaphor

The first approach to religious life, to language descriptive of it, and to ways of structuring it may be termed feudal (or medieval) inasmuch as it involves the first, negative and defensive, reaction to modernity, secularization, the Enlightenment society and culture, on the part of a Church still wedded to feudal embodiments of faith. It may also be termed Tridentine because historically it represents the Counter Reformation's refusal of the Reformers' critique of late medieval Catholicism, including monastic vows. In the broader history of the Church, magisterial actions such as the Syllabus of Errors of Pius IX, the anti-Modernist strictures of St. Pius X, and the encyclical *Humani Generis* of Pius XII in 1950 are some classic examples of this response. My LCWR Seminar essay describes several salient features of the world view enlivened by the organic metaphor: the primacy given to cosmic, anthropological, and ecclesiastical order, statically conceived within a traditional and non-evolutionary view of life strongly influenced by experience of the cycles of nature; a tendency to attend to abstract essences, and the understanding of change as the accidental modification of an enduring essence; the extension of the notion of *locus naturalis* (natural place) to ecclesiastical ranks and roles. Congruous with this world view was a strong sense of sacramentality and sacrality, with an accompanying accent on oaths, vows, consecration, permanency, and hierarchy. Further, the patriarchal assumptions of medieval society and culture led to an insistence on the inferiority and subordination of women to men.

Against this kind of background, there emerged the clear Tridentine teaching on the nature of religious life and its place in the Church. It was conceived as a fixed state in the Church, and described together with the episcopal state as a state of perfection, in contrast to the secular state, which was not. Its perfection was largely in the fact that through the three vows of poverty, perfect chastity, and obedience, it separated the religious from the threefold concupiscence in which lay the principal obstacles to charity, the essence of perfection. The higher way was the way of the three evangelical counsels, in contrast to the way of the commandments followed by seculars. Within the different types of religious life, the contemplative was more perfect than the active, and the mixed life more perfect than either (by the mixed life was meant not any combination of prayer and apostolate but the extension of contemplation through the proclamation of the word).

From another point of view, the religious state was a middle state, between the clerical and lay states. So far as authority was concerned, the Roman Pontiff was the highest superior of every religious. In general, monarchical rule, government by one person, tended to overcome earlier collegial forms of authority. Both in attitude and in ritual expression the life of religious obedience contained much that was feudal and sacral. The patriarchal element in this feudal model subordinated women to men in religious life, as generally in the Church.

For verification of the historical perseverance of this first approach to religious life even to our own day, one might cite the Code of Canon Law of 1918, and such commentaries as those of Cotel, Creusen-Ellis, Fanfani, and even Carpentier, which was intended to replace Cotel. This approach is not absent from Vatican II's chapter on religious life in the *Constitution on the Church,* and the *Decree on Religious Life.* One might also look to most pre-Vatican II Constitutions of religious orders and congregations of both men and women. What is more relevant to our situation in 1985 is to attend to its expression in the new law of the Church and the SCRIS "Essential Elements" interpretation of Church teaching. The language in these sources is particularly striking with respect to two themes: consecration and mission, and authority and autonomy. In both cases it is the organic metaphor, the feudal and Tridentine paradigm, which shapes the choice of language and accent. Without attempting an extensive analysis, I would instance the following as illustrative of this claim.

Regarding consecration and mission, both documents choose consecration (*vita consecrata*) as the basic term for describing not only religious life in the narrow canonical sense but also the life of secular Institutes. There is, further, a sharp contrast in both documents between secular Institutes and both monastic and apostolic religious communities. It is a major point of method, I believe, that both the new law and the SCRIS document work from a dyadic (secular and religious) rather than triadic (monastic, apostolic, secular) paradigm. The effect of such a choice is to blur the distinction of monastic and apostolic within the general category of consecrated life. The SCRIS document is quite consistent with this basic choice when it deals, for example, with apostolic mission only consequent upon its treatment of consecration by public vows and communion in community. This is a legitimate choice, but especially in view of the reluctance of the hierarchical Church in recent centuries, particularly in the case of women apostolic religious, to admit the legitimacy of apostolic life without major remnants of monastic cloister, it is fair to see in this choice a contemporary expression of a feudal and Tridentine outlook. We shall subsequently note the contrast of such a view with paradigms drawn from the mechanistic and artistic metaphors.

Respecting the theme of authority and autonomy, something similar is to be said. The prevailing concept of authority in the two magisterial documents is sacral, hierarchical, monarchical, and canonical, and the implicit anthropology on which it is based is clearly feudal and not modern in character. The autonomy of religious Institutes is formally asserted in both documents, but other statements tend to negate or weaken this assertion. Authority is conceived within narrow limits as the power to rule descending from God to the hierarchy, specifically the Roman Pontiff, the supreme superior of each religious, and thence into the particular community through the person of the major superior.

In contrast to paradigms drawn from the second and third metaphors, there is no acknowledgment of any authority present in a religious community prior to its formal recognition and the acceptance of its constitutions by the official Church. In addition, all apostolic activity on the part of religious appears to fall under the need of a hierarchical mandate. So far as the exercise of authority within the community is concerned, the tilt of the new law and of the SCRIS document is clearly toward the major superior. It is acknowledged that the general chapter also exercises supreme authority, but this concession is immediately qualified by such characterizations as "in an extraordinary manner," "while it is in session," and "an *ad hoc* body" whose members "ordinarily meet together for one chapter only" (n. 51). It is significant that in both documents the role of major superior is treated prior to the role of the general chapter. The notion that major superiors are accountable to the membership through the general chapter is completely absent. And the SCRIS document accents that "chapters should not be invoked so frequently as to interfere with the good functioning of the ordinary authority of the major superior" (norm 48).

Underlying such specific prescriptions is a conception of religious life in its authority and structures which tends toward homogeneity with the authority and structures of the hierarchical Church as such. The structures of religious life are said to "reflect the Christian hierarchy of which the head is Christ himself" (n. 49).

When all these provisions are taken together, it is clear that the SCRIS document deals with the perennial tension between religious charism and ecclesiastical recognition and direction with a bias toward the latter. And to the degree that religious Institutes, both clerical and lay, are drawn in this document toward a distinctive place within the hierarchical structure of the Church, one may discern a clericalizing tendency at work. Confirming this perception is a curious particular: the *Constitution on the Church* of Vatican II had insisted both that the religious state was not a middle one between the clerical and lay states (n. 43) and that the religious life did not belong to the hierarchical structure of the Church (n. 44). Two decades later we find the SCRIS document interpreting this teaching with the statement, "Religious life has *its own place* in relation to the divine and hierarchical structure of the Church" (n. 38; italics added).

In summary, the organic root metaphor, particularly as expressed in the historical mindsets of sacrality, hierarchical order, and monarchy, has found fresh expression in some salient provisions of the new law of the Church and particularly of the SCRIS document. As we proceed to identify and illustrate the other two metaphors, we can better understand recent American-Roman tensions as well as the language options taken by CMSM in recent phases of its journey.

2. Religious Life in the Mechanistic Metaphor

The second approach to religious life, based on the mechanistic root metaphor, reflects a broader accommodation of the Church to the world of the Enlightenment. Since it shares in the pluralism characteristic of modernity, it is less susceptible to neat formulation than the Tridentine or feudal approach. As a general current it began to emerge in the early nineteenth century. Pius IX was originally hailed as "the liberal Pope," and Leo XIII, especially in his encyclical on the working class in 1891, showed how accommodation was working even at the top. Despite recurring setbacks, and thanks to a variety of pioneers like Maurice Blondel, M.-J. Lagrange, and Pierre Teilhard de Chardin, along with later figures like Chenu and Congar, Karl Rahner, Lonergan, and Murray, a firm beachhead was secured within the Church's intellectual life, especially in the period before and during Vatican II. The Council, while it did not put an end to the feudal reaction to modernity, does represent an official acceptance of some of the key insights and values of modernity. Vatican II's documents on revelation (preceded by *Divino Afflante* in 1943), religious freedom, and the Church in the modern world exemplify the somewhat halting and ambiguous entry of modernity into the mainstream of Roman Catholic life.

Some of the broad features of this viewpoint which have shaped the second approach to religious life may be listed: philosophically, an ability to live with and even to prize doubt as a mark of enlightenment; acknowledgment of the validity of human experience (expressed in conflicting philosophical views such as existentialism, personalism, empiricism, pragmatism, phenomenology, etc.); attentiveness to process rather than to stable substances, and the desire to interpret the world through the concepts of evolution, relativity, and indeterminism. Freud, Jung, and the entire psychoanalytical movement disclosed the influence of the unconscious on personal and social behavior. Comparable changes took place in the fields of economics, sociology, and political science, as the industrial and political revolutions of modern times led to individualism, nationalism, and the various stages and forms of capitalism. One does not have to be a classical Marxist to appreciate how, very close to the center of this development, the machine tended to displace the land, as source of the dominant metaphor for industrial society.

In such a context it was only to be expected that, in the Church's grudging accommodation to industrial society, both the language and the structures of religious life would begin to heed the voices of change. A shift of accent from the contemplative to the active, from separation from the world to involvement in the world, from consecration to mission, prophecy, and service, began to appear as our century progressed. Recourse to changing human experience as a privileged place of encounter with God raised questions about traditional definitions of religious life based on a preoccupation with abstract essences. The Enlightenment's cherishing of individual freedom and of human rights, as well as distress over the acquiescence of Christians in totalitarian oppression, brought a less passive and less sacral understanding of the vow of obedience. The modern world's bias toward democracy challenged the Tridentine bias toward monarchy. The secularization characteristic of the modern world, at the point at which it prompted a secular reading of the Gospel, brought a movement away from sacral language and models for the vowed life. The term "celibacy" tended to replace "virginity" and "perfect chastity" in describing the second vow (the latter term now being seen as pejorative in its implications for the chastity of married people). A sense of historicity reduced the tendency to see religious life as an enduring form or essence, and relativized and desacralized the notion of permanent consecration through the vows. Models of the Church shaped in large part by democratic biases against elitism brought a new insistence on the baptismal call to holiness and mission, contrasting with the traditional "state of perfection" understanding of religious life.

It is obvious that this Enlightenment view has found abundant expression not only in the more progressive theological literature and

Chapter documents of the past few decades, but also in official Church documents. For example, the *Constitution on the Church* is at pains to affirm that the profession of the counsels is beneficial to development of the person (n. 46). It denies that religious are useless citizens of the earthly city (n. 46). As we have seen, it insists that religious are not a middle group between clergy and laity (n. 43), and that religious do not belong to the hierarchical structure of the Church (n. 44). The decree on religious life of Vatican II calls for the adaptation of living, praying, and working to physical and psychological conditions, to the needs of the apostolate, to the requirements of a given culture, and to social and economic conditions (n. 3). The brilliant formula, *"accommodata renovatio,"* likewise reflects a sense of urgent need for significant change (n. 2). Religious are to be educated to the prevailing manners of contemporary society (n. 18). Both in the new law of the Church and in the SCRIS document, side by side with Tridentine language, liberal formulations find a voice. The new law, for example, acknowledges a rightful autonomy of life, especially in governance, for institutes of consecrated life (n. 586). It is clear, then, that neither the new law of the Church governing religious life nor the SCRIS document may be described as simply or totally perpetuating a feudal model of religious life. This leaves open the question, of course, of the relative weight of the two root metaphors in these documents.

3. Religious Life in the Artistic Metaphor

The third approach to religious life, based on an artistic metaphor, is even more difficult than the second to define by means of specific philosophical or cultural ideas. Because it is in an incipient stage of influence, it does not admit of the same kind of verification in past or present history as the Tridentine and Enlightenment approaches.

The artistic root metaphor is a potential source for a wide variety of specific paradigms, depending on what is singled out as crucial in the interpretation of history, e.g., work and production, or the family and relationships between the sexes, or the situation of humans within the earthly and cosmic environment. It is, furthermore, holistic and comprehensive, more interested in integration than in disjunction. In this it contrasts with the mechanistic metaphor, as the artist contrasts with the mechanic in sensitivity to wholeness.

It needs further to be said that while the three metaphors, and the paradigms inspired by them, are decidedly different, there are points at which any two of them will contrast with the third. Both the organic and artistic metaphors, for example, ground a critical stance toward the individualism, progressivism, and evolutionism which has been historically associated with the dominance of the mechanistic metaphor. It takes a discerning judgment to single out, in criticisms made of the liberal society in Church circles, which criticisms are nostalgic and reactionary and which call to a future not yet experienced.

Here, then, are some of the features which distinguish a post-Enlightenment conception based on the artistic metaphor. Its philosophical affinities are with modes of thought critical of the idealism, existentialism, personalism, secularism, individualism, and pluralism characteristic of Western society in our times. Marxism and other varieties of socialist and communitarian thought provide this approach with strong convictions regarding (1) the societal or political character of the whole of human life, (2) the place of dialectic and conflict as positive and dynamic forces in history, (3) a certain priority of experience and praxis over theory, and (4) the key role of the most deprived groups, named as the proletariat, the powerless, or the poor, in effecting change in society. In theology, it has been political and liberation theologies, especially those stemming from struggles for social, economic, racial and sexual liberation, together with such ecological and cosmic theologies as those of Teilhard de Chardin and Thomas Berry, that have intimated what a Christian version of the artistic metaphor might look like. Acknowledging the advances made in the liberal society of the West, these currents tend to be critical of that society's individualism, its secularism, its exaggerated cultivation of specialization, its tendency to "privatize" religious faith, its proclivity toward a bland evolutionism and developmentalism, its avoidance of the eschatological and apocalyptical aspects of the Gospel, and its spawning of a bourgeois or middle class brand of civil religion which in effect makes the Church a captive within the dominant technological culture.

Among the alternative visions and strategies which help to identify this third position are (1) a retrieval of the political character of the Gospel and of Christian witness and ministry, (2) a reduction of the Enlightenment Church's dichotomy between evangelization and human development/liberation, (3) a related reduction of the sharp distinctions between clergy and laity, and between religious and seculars, in the evangelizing mission of the Church, (4) movement from a *Volkskirche,* that is, an institutional Church in service to a largely middle class membership, toward a people's Church, a base community Church centered sociologically around the poor and ecclesiologically around baptism and not orders, (5) the need for a "preferential option for the poor" and the espousal of the "hermeneutical privilege of the poor" as the key pastoral strategy for our times, and (6) a return, after the Enlightenment Church's somewhat bland cultivation of creation and incarnation, to an insistence on the cross, on conflict, on the need to uncover and resist evil, and on a non-violent response to structural evil in both Church and society.

If one looks for approaches to religious life which embody this emerging artistic metaphor, I would suggest especially an examination of some of the notable Chapter documents of communities of women religious in the United States. Johannes Metz' *Followers of Christ,* especially when read in conjunction with his *The Emerging Church,* and several of Rosemary Haughton's writings, exemplify theological versions of this approach.

A summary view of religious life as seen from the standpoint of the artistic metaphor would run somewhat as follows: Religious life, in the traditional sense, is to be identified only on the basis of history and not on the basis of abstract definitions. Its canonical description, though inevitable and helpful, is derivative from its theological understanding, particularly of those who experience it from within. Further, religious life is to be situated within the life of baptismal communities, all of which are called to the fullness of discipleship and to the transformation of the world in the spirit of the beatitudes. No adequate distinction can be made between the life of the commandments and the life of the counsels. Every semblance of elitism based on the call to celibacy is to be repudiated. God will doubtless continue to call some Christians, though possibly in smaller numbers, to constitute celibate communities in a wide variety of forms, but such communities will live, witness, and serve always within the larger community of discipleship. If some such communities symbolize in a special way the contemplative or eschatological dimensions of all Christian life, they do so not as substitutes but as representatives. Further, action is not derivative from contemplation; rather, the relationship is reciprocal, and all genuine human and Christian action is inseparably both contemplative and responsive in character.

Similarly, in this third approach, the dignity, responsibility, and legitimate autonomy of the individual, of small groups, and of whole communities with respect to the hierarchical Church is affirmed, but the individualism which tended to inhere in Enlightenment versions of autonomy in the period of breaking out from feudal confinements is now challenged. This challenge, however, takes the form not of a reversion to authoritarian structures but rather of recourse to decisional processes based on the theology and spirituality of the communal discernment of spirits. The notions of autonomy, participation, and subsidiarity, gained in the Enlightenment model, are penetrated in a post-Enlightenment model with a new insistence on the common good, perceived however on the basis of an artistic, not an organic, root metaphor.

It should not be thought that communal discernment functions as an alternative to doubt and conflict. No less than the second approach, the radical view believes that doubt and conflict can be creative. But now a non-violent communal response tends to overshadow insistence on individual rights in dealing with conflict.

This same expectation of conflict and adherence to non-violence in resolving conflict is carried over to the understanding of the ecclesial character of religious life. Within the artistic root metaphor, less need is seen for hierarchical control of the life and ministry of religious. Where the charismatic and autonomous character of these voluntary communities is taken seriously, the basic norms of subsidiarity and participation will leave to the communities themselves primary responsibility for their life and ministry. There is nothing in the nature of this way of Christian life which requires that canonical approbation carry with it the degree of control exercised in our times by Roman authorities. This by no means says that religious communities need not be, like all Christians, obedient to legitimate authority. But, consistent with the Church's social teaching, it does call for a major disengagement on the part of the hierarchical Church from attitudes and structures of authority appropriate perhaps within a feudal paradigm, or even within an Enlightenment one, but not within this more radical one.

Finally, it may be possible to symbolize the differences among the three approaches by referring to the three traditional vows. The feudal approach may be said to accent *obedience* because of its preoccupation with the orderly passage of authority from God to the hierarchy to the person of the major superior. Within such a paradigm poverty is assimilated to obedience by the accent on the so-called poverty of dependence, and perfect chastity is understood according to a moral theology which is congruous with the sacral and hierarchical image of human life, consisting in the subordination of bodily drives to spiritual control. Thus the hierarchical order of obedience permeates the understanding of all three vows. In the famous Ignatian image of Jesuit obedience, the lowermost is governed by the middlemost, and the middlemost by the highermost.

In the liberal approach the vow of *celibacy* appears to be primary because of the strong personalistic accent of Enlightenment spirituality. The personal fulfillment of the individual religious through a celibately chaste exercise of affectivity and sexuality both within the community and in ministry is here highlighted. Not only celibacy, but poverty and obedience as well, are interpreted through this prism of individual human development.

The radical approach seems to hold out as primary the vow of poverty, understood as a shared preferential option for the poor of the world; both celibacy and obedience are interpreted from the standpoint of this option.

A final word on the three paradigms before moving to a reflection on the essays of the present volume. In describing the first approach I have singled out in the new law of the Church and in the SCRIS document two themes: authority/autonomy and consecration/mission. The descriptions of the second and third approaches have sufficiently, I hope, indicated how they are inclined to speak to the former tension. Their respective positions regarding consecration/mission may be briefly described as follows. The Enlightenment paradigm, strongly influenced by historical secularization and by various philosophies of action, would tend both to install the concept of mission as normative and to desacralize the notion of consecration to the point of seeing the traditional "separation from the world" as outdated language, at least for communities of apostolic religious. Terms like "covenant" and "commitment" are more congenial to this outlook than "consecration." The third paradigm would endorse this disengagement from the sacralistic connotations of the first paradigm, and would likewise insist on the primacy of mission. Its difference from the second paradigm might be said to consist in a stronger accent on the communal dimensions of mission. Both of these paradigms would find in the setting apart of Paul and Silas for ministry (Acts 13:2) a symbolic base for their insistence that, for apostolic religious, there is no setting apart *from* the world but, on the contrary, a setting apart *toward* the world.

III

In reflecting on the previous essays of this volume, and on the CMSM journey which they exhibit, I must forego systematic comment on particular essays. Nor will I attempt any kind of synthesis, especially because more than one of the essays are synthetic in character. Instead, I will sort out several important themes which appear in the essays, and comment on them from the standpoint of the three root metaphors. This will lead to some brief concluding observations on the role of leadership in the years ahead. It will be clear that my personal biases are with the third approach to religious life. But my chief intent is to raise further questions for reflection.

1. *Understanding and Interpreting the Journey*

Does the paradigm of the three root metaphors throw light on the historical experience of U.S. men religious, especially as this journey has been here portrayed by John Padberg and David Fleming? I believe that it does. It affords a perspective from which we can appreciate both the achievements and the limitations of those who have gone before us. When Padberg writes of "the institutionalization of a frontier charism," and Fleming of "frontier deeds and base camp thoughts," they are using a distinctively American language in order to portray what happened when the feudal Church, precisely through its most charismatic communities, sought to inculturate the Gospel in successive stages of the Americanization of the Roman Catholic Church. No detailed characterization of that inculturation beyond what these two authors have given is possible here. But I would venture the broad statement that what happened overall was an accommodation of the feudal/Tridentine paradigm to a cultural scene which invited and even pressured the American Church toward an Enlightenment model. In both the resistance and the accommodation to an alien culture, secular and Protestant, women and men religious played a variety of key roles. Despite the risk of building Procrustean beds to explain our history, the paradigms inspired by the three root metaphors can serve in its interpretation. For example, John Padberg's observation that the institutionalization of charism, while finding community support, was largely the work of outstanding individuals may serve as an example of Roman Catholic accommodation to the individualism of the Enlightenment society. In any case we may say that, at least prior to the past few decades, the drama and tension and ambiguity of U.S. men religious has been found in the task of assisting the passage of the American Church from the first to the second root metaphors. Just how this broad statement would need to be nuanced and specified, for example in language about religious vows, or in shaping intramural structures, must be left to interested readers to pursue.

2. Laity and Clerics

A more specific theme within the interpretation of our journey would deal with conceptions and practices regarding the various vocations in the Church. Several of the previous essays touch upon the lay/cleric relationship in passing, but only the essay on clericalism—which, incidentally, may deserve to rank as a landmark in CMSM history—highlights it. A partial explanation of this relatively scant attention to a major sign of the times may be found in the preoccupation found in religious communities of the past few decades with finding an adequate statement of their distinctive role in the Church. To the extent to which this has been a search for a clear and distinct definition of religious life, the feudal root metaphor has been at work. In any case the question I wish to raise is whether, given the membership of both clerical and lay communities with CMSM, the framework of the three root metaphors can be enlightening. Historically, the Tridentine model of a Church composed of clerics, religious and laity, in an order of increasing marginality, seems to have prevailed for well over a century until the Vatican II era. As long as American Catholicism saw itself as an embattled minority within a basically Protestant culture, we were in no position to learn from the other Christian Churches what they had learned about the call of all the baptized to holiness and ministry. Once the waves of Catholic immigration and urban settlement provided the basic pastoral problematic for the Cath-

olic Church, we were largely cut off from earlier examples of a vig-
orously active laity. The coming of age of American Catholics within
our century, the ecumenical movement, the vocational crisis of clerics
and religious, and the teaching of Vatican II on the call of all the baptized to holiness and mission have all combined to heighten our consciousness of this major sign of the times, the emergence of the laity
in the life and ministry of the Church.

The theme of the empowerment of the laity as a primary imperative for the ministry of clergy and religious may not be as strongly
represented in this volume as it is among many U.S. men religious.
This is not the place to explore the implications of this imperative.
But I would ask two reflective questions.

First, assuming that CMSM membership as a whole has moved
beyond the feudal paradigm of strongly hierarchized laity-clergy and
secular-religious relationships, where does the membership stand regarding the prevalence of the mechanistic or the artistic metaphor as
applied to these relationships? My surmise is that the majority would
be dealing with these relationships on the basis of the mechanistic root
metaphor, and would not yet have embraced the radicality of a viewpoint centered in the basic pastoral community. We have, for example, accommodated the traditional relationships found in Third
Orders and Sodalities while still leaving lay spirituality in a derivative
position. And while it has become commonplace to link the vows of
religious with baptismal vows, the prevailing tendency is to see religious life as not only distinctive but as in some fashion unique. The
"sea change" described by John Coleman, involving a paradigm shift
from an ecclesiology based on orders to one based on baptism, with
both clerics and religious having now to find their distinctive roles
only within an egalitarian model of Christian life and ministry, seems
to me to be in its early stages, if I accurately grasp what is being said
in these essays.

A second question is posed in ignorance of the relevant history
within CMSM of lay-clerical relationships. Given the fact that
CMSM unites in one organization both lay and clerical Institutes, including some Institutes whose membership comprises both laymen
and clerics, does the comparison and contrast of the second and third
root metaphors suggest directions for growth of the organization?
More specifically, does the presence of lay members within the ranks
of CMSM point, both symbolically and pragmatically, to a special call

to CMSM regarding the empowerment of the laity in today's Church? If such empowerment actually is or might easily become a primary objective of CMSM, how might reflection on the root metaphors serve in conceiving desired directions?

3. *Justice, the Middle Class, and the Poor*

Here again the question to explore has to do with a comparison of the perspectives of the second and third root metaphors. That CMSM's membership has listened and assented both to magisterial teaching and to liberation theology regarding justice, the option for the poor, and the need for global structural change is beyond question. The inter-American dialogues as well as collaboration with LCWR, notably the Convergence experience in Cleveland in 1978, have been influential in this regard. We might be tempted to conclude that, at least with respect to this complexus of questions, CMSM stands wholly within the third metaphor. That such a conclusion would be too facile is part of the service rendered by John Grindel's challenging essay in this volume. It strikingly illustrates that third metaphor models and paradigms, listened to from within the second metaphor, can evoke a response notably different from and even in some tension with responses from within the third metaphor itself. To say this is to signalize the difference, not to stigmatize the response. And my observations are to be taken not with respect to his statement of goals for the U.S. Church but only with respect to his proposed strategies for achieving these goals.

Why do I suggest that John Grindel's response lies within the second, and not the third metaphor? On the one hand he passionately espouses the language of liberation, the option for the poor, and the need for radical change of global structures. This language, we have seen, emerges from the post-Enlightenment way of thinking. But when he comes to proposing strategies for such change, it seems to me that he has recourse to a liberal outlook, which is precisely what the radical viewpoint of liberation theology is calling into question. His proposed strategies call for (1) proclamation of the word as the one task of the Church, through which everything else is to be viewed, (2) the middle class in the United States as primary audience for such proclamation, and (3) the media as *the* means through which the power of the middle class is to be, as he says, manipulated. Now all three components of this strategy are in contrast with the language and strategies characteristic of third metaphor thinking: (1) not simply proclamation of the word to a chosen audience but reflection on the word, coupled with grassroots social analysis, on the part of basic communities; (2) not primarily the middle class but the poor themselves as subjects and agents of their own liberation; (3) not the skilled use of the media, which in their fostering of illusion and numbness are a primary symbol of what is oppressive in the present culture, but evangelization of the whole Church and of society conducted by the poor who are "hermeneutically privileged." These would appear to be the pastoral priorities which emerge from an analysis of today's situation in the light of the third root metaphor. Obviously, this does not deny that the present U.S. Church and its ministry needs to evangelize or catechize the middle class, both because the Church itself in its membership and leadership is, numerically and ideologically, a middle class Church, and because without the conversion of significant segments of the middle class the empowerment of the poor and the eventual transformation of structures cannot happen. Nor need we discountenance a carefully discerned use of the media, aware of the risks and ambiguities which this involves. But what a third metaphor approach would question is whether the primary engagement of the ministerial energies of U.S. men religious need be or should be in a ministry of the word to the middle class through the media. An alternative strategy calls for consideration: the prudent but firm and extensive redeployment of energies so that the primary focus becomes the direct empowerment of the poor through the formation of basic communities among them. In any case, and however the question ought to be put, I am saying that John Grindel's essay can be most fruitfully read within the framework of the root metaphors.

4. Institutions and Prophetic Ministry

Another area where the root metaphor approach can be serviceable to leadership among men religious has to do with the relationship between prophecy and institution. Several studies in the present volume testify to the presence in CMSM consciousness of a lively sense of the importance of structures and institutions for faith and evangelization. That third metaphor thinking has taken place within CMSM is indicated by the conviction, which is repeated several times, that our prophetic role as religious calls us to be critical of institutions, secular or ecclesiastical, at the point at which they either become oppressive of persons and communities or are manifestly too cumbersome as vehicles for Christian witness and service. In a similar vein, John Lozano's section on the choice of life over institution aptly portrays the presence of a "sort of diffuse Franciscanism in our times," a mood which is skeptical of the value and Christian efficacy of apostolic institutions. There appears, then, to be a broad consensus within CMSM that prophetic freedom needs to be exercised today with respect to all institutions.

But this broad consensus leaves unresolved a more specific set of questions. These have to do with continuing engagement in or calculated disengagement from institutional ministries, particularly the ministry of education (men religious by and large do not face the even greater challenges posed to women religious engaged in institutional health care). John Padberg's historical survey signalizes the importance over two centuries of "the building up of an infrastructure of institutions." He also derives a lesson for the future from the fact that sometimes apostolates instituted by individual entrepreneurs often "faltered or produced far less results than might have been expected" because they were not sufficiently institutionalized. He probably speaks here for the wisdom of experience of many major superiors. But David Fleming points to the shadow side of this conviction when he comments that "too many religious communities of men in the United States are still fearful to evaluate their institutional commitments; and in the face of declining and aging personnel, many of them cling uncritically to works which exhaust their manpower and crush hope of creativity. Such a lack of flexibility, if it continues, will be quite devastating in the decade ahead as the full impact of our recent lack of recruitment hits us."

The question for assessment here is not the abstract question of whether the Gospel can and should be embodied in graced institutions, but rather: What is it time for now, by way of attitude and strategy? Some would see the question as otiose, given the decline of membership coupled with widespread anti-institutional attitudes on the part of the young. Still, leadership has important choices to make. They are not made easier by the fact that, so far as I know, we lack adequate criteria and tools for evaluating our complex apostolic institutions, especially in the field of higher education.

In this quandary, what the root metaphor approach can contribute is a heightening of attention to the assumptions behind contrasting attitudes and strategies. I would say two things. First, commitment to institutional ministry, especially within the field of education, has been characteristic of American men religious as a major aspect of the accommodation of their charisms to the secular culture of the Enlightenment. It has stood squarely within the second root metaphor, and perhaps has been based, at least within the present century, on a "Christ within culture" model of evangelization. Second, to the extent to which the third root metaphor distances itself from the second, and disengages from the prevailing middle class culture of our country, it tends to view corporate involvement in existing institutions—again, especially in the field of higher education—as a dissipation of precious apostolic energies which might be more creatively engaged in breaking new trails. This does not imply that the third metaphor encourages a shift from societal to interpersonal attitudes. On the contrary, it is, as we have seen, acutely sensitive to the importance of institutions, sinful and graced, in shaping life. It differs from the second metaphor both by forging a closer link between the interpersonal and the societal and by bringing a Christian analysis to bear on all structures and institutions. Its reluctance to continue corporate investment in apostolic institutions which represent an accommodation of prophecy to the established secular culture stems principally from its negative appraisal of that culture. One may not simply equate adherence to the third metaphor with a disinclination to continue institutional apostolates, or vice versa. Still, an initial critical stance toward such continuation is more typical of the third than of the second metaphor.

5. *Communion, Solidarity, Friendship*

If, to use John Lozano's phrase again, a "sort of diffuse Franciscanism in our times" asserts itself in prioritizing life over institutions, it finds a distinct but related expression in a theme which is voiced several times these essays. The theme is variously expressed— as *communion and solidarity* ("Pilgrims and Prophets"), as *fellowship* (Alan McCoy), as the *community of men and women* (the clericalism paper), and as *affectio* (Peter Henriot). The themes of *prophecy* and *discipleship,* highlighted especially by David Fleming and John Lozano, lend themselves to integration with this accent on the interpersonal. It is the creation and development of prophetic communities of disciples of Jesus, not the preservation or reform of the structures and institutions which serve to safeguard such communities, which appears to crystallize the predominant call to U.S. men religious today. An expression coined by John Haughey a decade ago, "the conspiracy of God," points to the most central experience of such communities: con-spiring, that is, breathing together from the gift of the Spirit of love.

This singling out, as the final word, of friendship and affection might appear to be an option for the second metaphor which, I have suggested, makes celibacy pivotal among the vows of religious. I think, rather, that what is seeking expression here is an understanding of friendship which has transcended the second metaphor's somewhat apolitical handling of friendship, and its proclivity to keep personal relationships and commitment to public justice and peace separate from each other. The conspiracy I speak of now is a gathering of friends, of sisters and brothers, around a prophetic mission conceived in terms of the furthering of the reign of God in history through the empowerment of the poor.

Some of the base communities among the poor in Latin America foreshadow what is here envisaged. But North American versions will be fed also by some quite different currents. When the empowerment of women in Church and society, and the empowerment of the laity of the Church, are assumed as major pastoral objectives by U.S. men religious, the friendship and solidarity of which we are here speaking goes beyond any relationships possible within the perspective of the second root metaphor. It becomes very clear that a future in friendship, especially as portrayed in the CMSM paper on clericalism, has nothing to do with the clubmanship of clerics which all of us have known in the past. I would suggest, finally, that the Gospel scenario which best fits this vision of the future is Jesus sitting at table in the house of the publican Levi, become Matthew, surrounded by those who constituted the poor of his culture.

By way of conclusion I would suggest three lessons which official leadership of religious communities might draw from the preceding reflection.

First, it is important that leaders learn, by practice, to engage themselves and others not only in social analysis in general but precisely in cultural analysis. Beneath political, economic, and social structures, both secular and ecclesiastical, which affect the life and ministry of each religious community, lies a more powerful and less accessible world of myth and symbol, dream and affect. If the breathing together which constitutes the life of a religious community is to have depth and staying power in our present apocalyptic age, the world of culture must become a primary area of contemplation and discerning reflection.

Second, a valuable gift in religious leadership today is the power to estimate at what stage of transition from first to second or from second to third root metaphors a particular community or segments within it stands, to grasp the salient features of the journey which have led to such a point, and to be sensitive to the forces which have either blocked forward movement or induced deviation from a path of genuine growth. Thus the paradigm of the three root metaphors can help the religious leader as a tool for interpreting the history of his order or congregation.

Third, most important of all, perhaps, is the development in religious leaders of that self-knowledge which puts them in touch with the influence of root metaphors on their own attitudes and behavior. Even the saints fail to achieve perfect consistency, because the life project of embodying the Gospel in culture encounters many obstacles from our own sinfulness and from the sin of the world. But a consistent effort at reflective appropriation of one's own personal inculturation of the Gospel, leading to significant choices regarding the style and forms of inculturation, is both possible and necessary if religious leadership is to be both wise and prophetic.

AFTERWORD

Ron Carignan, O.M.I.

Ron Carignan, O.M.I. is President of the Conference of Major Superiors of Men of the United States.

The image of crossroads in the title of this book well describes our present situation as men religious in the United States. We seem to find ourselves at a critical point of intersection on the road we have been traveling for the past twenty years or so. We can look back with satisfaction at a difficult stretch of road knowing that we were not simply caught up in aimless wandering. We can also look ahead at the road opening up before us, fully aware that the present moment is one of decision. In this afterword, I would like to reflect briefly on the road we have traveled, the challenge of the present moment and the road we seek to enter.

THE ROAD WE HAVE TRAVELED

The past twenty years have been difficult years. When the fathers of the Second Vatican Council realized that the world was caught up in a "real social and cultural transformation whose repercussions are felt on the religious level" and urged us as religious "to be prompt in performing the renewal task allotted to us in the Church today," they ushered in a totally new experience for all of us. We entered into a profound and dramatic time of transition, significant new values emerged, and familiar values were transformed. In fact we experienced a major shift in consciousness.

The time of transition we have been living through is profound in that it has touched our very understanding and living of religious life in rather startling ways, dramatic in that in the history of Christianity such a transition has been experienced only four, possibly five times, during the past two thousand years. It was certainly a first for us as U.S. religious. We were often bewildered by the signs of death. It was difficult for us to conceptualize this type of change. For a number of years we were preoccupied by the signs of death and we plodded

190

through the unavoidable grieving stages of denial, bargaining, anger and depression. But we were moving into a new land, and we began to experience a newness within ourselves evidenced in a broader global and ecclesial attitude with a fresh interest in justice and peace issues. New value words found their places in our conversations and documents, words such as Gospel/liberation, faith/risk, solidarity with the poor, poverty/simplicity, obedience/mutual accountability, integration/wholeness. When we talked about our vision of the Church we underlined such values as interdependence, unity/diversity, dialogue, discipleship of equals and enculturation.

Important shifts occurred around major elements in the living of our religious life. Community was no longer seen primarily as a way of living out a common observance but, rather as a way of sharing life. Ministry was talked about less and less in terms of common apostolates and more and more as an expression of a corporate sense of mission. Our understanding of authority expanded to include authority of persons and authority of community as well as authority of office. All of this led us to a critical shift in consciousness. Truly we perceive the world and the church differently than we did some twenty or so years ago. We see ourselves functioning within these realities in vastly different ways and there are important new needs to which we are trying to respond.

THE PRESENT MOMENT

A useful way of characterizing the present moment is to see it as a search for integration on both the individual and corporate levels. Integration has to do with the basic quality of possessing an effective internal balance as well as being in harmony with the environment. It is a condition that favors life. The present search for integration follows two lines of action. The first has to do with finding one's spiritual center both as groups and as individuals. The other involves a sufficient grasp of the global/ecclesial/cultural context within which religious life is presently struggling to be life-giving.

To find one's spiritual center is to be in touch with the core value in which the sense of self finds its deepest meaning and from which it derives its vital energy. At our 1983 CMSM Assembly we dealt with the topic: *Our Search for God as U.S. Men Religious.* I do believe this was a significant topic related to our search for integration. We became more and more conscious of this search for God as the core of our religious existence as individual religious and as communities. We saw that all other symbols in our lives sought to unify and mediate this central reality. Related to this search for integration is a new urgency I find among many religious congregations to recover a shared sense of common purpose. This is certainly an appropriate agenda for many communities at this time.

Our 1984 CMSM Assembly sought to be a moment of convergence in our struggle to understand the context in which we seek to live as religious. The theme, *U.S. Men Religious, Formed by the Culture, Challenged by the Gospel, Called To Proclaim the Kingdom,* focused on the global, ecclesial, and cultural reality that is ours as U.S. men religious. We ended with many questions—questions we will continue to brood over for a long time. How resourceful we are in addressing these questions will greatly influence how we will walk together in the road ahead.

THE ROAD AHEAD

To a large degree, the road ahead is largely unknown. God is always full of surprises. We do know, however, that we will have to deal with smaller numbers and with an aging population of men religious. Possibly our greatest challenge in the road ahead will be to walk it with integrity. In a Spirit-filled time of discernment we have discovered significant new values. We must make choices based on these values. A new vision of Church is beginning to take shape among us as men religious. We cannot attempt to escape from the vulnerability in which we are placing ourselves by espousing such a vision. There is always the temptation to turn back and seek security in the past, to seek to control rather than to relate. Possibly our greatest gift to the Church will be by way of serious and persistent dialogue, one that hears and dignifies differences while being committed to fundamental unity. I do believe that a strong commitment to dialogue can go a long way in freeing up the prophetic in the Church. If we can move in this direction, I have no doubt that the road ahead will be a real life-giving trip.